War Stories

BOOKS BY LEW LEBLANC

War Stories
  Some Memories from the Firehouse Years

Firefighter War Stories II
  More Memories from the Firehouse Years

War Stories

Some Memories from the Firehouse Years

Lew LeBlanc

Edited and Illustrated by Sue LeBlanc

Copyright © 2014, 2018 Lew LeBlanc

Illustrated and edited by Sue LeBlanc

All rights reserved. This book or any portion thereof may not be reproduced or transmitted in any form or by any means, electrical or mechanical, including photocopying, recording, or by an information storage and retrieval system—except for the use of brief quotations in a book review or scholarly journal—without the express written permission of the publisher.

Although the author and publisher have made every effort to ensure the accuracy and completeness of information contained in this book, we assume no responsibility for errors, inaccuracies, omissions, or any inconsistency herein. All opinions expressed in this book are those of the author.

Andremily Tree Publishing, Natick, Massachusetts
www.FirefighterWarStories.com

Printed and bound in the United States of America.

First Printing, 2014

Third edition, Georgia font

ISBN 978-0-692-28969-3

Dedication

This work is dedicated to the men and women of the fire service everywhere, who do the job every day because they love it.

Contents

Acknowledgements i
Introduction 1

The Stories

30 Minutes, Guaranteed 5
26F 7
Afraid of the Uniform 9
After You! 10
Air Horn 12
Ambulance Account 13
Amusement Park 15
At Home In Any Firehouse 17
Auto Body Shop 18
Baby 20
Bad Ass 22
Barns 23
Belt Buckle 26
Bottled Water 28
Brush 29
Buddy Breathers 31
Burn Permits 36
Burning Books 38
Canine Arrest 40
Carbon Monoxide 42
Chop Saw 44
City at a Standstill 45

Confession Time	47
Cows	49
CPR Card	50
Crematorium	52
Did We Lose Something?	53
Didn't Speak All Day	54
Dispatch	55
Down Vest	57
The Dragon Escapes	59
Drive from Maine	61
Drowning	63
Eight Inches of Cold Steel	65
Eternal Thanks to Those Cops	66
Expensive Phone Call	68
Faith in the Guys	69
Falling Asleep on the Throne	71
Father's Day	72
Fire from Hell	73
Fireball	76
First CPR	79
Floods	81
Gas Explosion	84
Get the Bolt Cutters	85
Get the Scoop	87
Good Stop	89
The Great Outdoors	91
Ground Fog	93
Gumby Suit	95
HAV Valve	96

Hawk Eye 97
Hiding the Dog 98
Hometown 100
Hornets 102
I Know the Way Out 104
I Rode the Step 106
I Work In Car 108
Ice Rescue 110
It Ain't For Everybody 113
It's All Greek to Me 115
Key in the Rock 116
Last Support Fire 118
Lawn Ornament Fire 120
Locks Were Made for Honest People 121
Long Lug Out 122
Malfunctioning Smokes 124
A Man I Used to Know 125
Memories 129
MFFA Car Fires 131
Mongolians 132
Most Rewarding Day 133
Neck Breather 135
Never Mind That. Just Do It! 136
New Building 137
New Tools and Gadgetry 140
No Pole 143
No Protection 144
No Stipend 146
No Thank Yous 148

No Ventilation 149

No Water on Magnesium Fires 151

Oh Man, That Hurt! 152

Old Enough to Buy 154

Old Habits 155

One of Our Own 156

Only One House?! 158

Oops…Wrong Town! 161

Paint Brushes 162

Painted Toenails 163

Panic 164

Partners 166

Plane Crash 170

Public Outcry 171

Rescue at the Bridge 174

Rhoids 176

SAED 177

Santa's Eyebrows 179

Sausages on the Stove 180

School Fire Drills 182

Section 12s 185

Shish-ka-bob 189

Shut Up and Do Your Job! 192

Slip and Slide 194

Someone I Knew 196

Sometimes You Just Have to Wonder, But You Can't Cure Stupid 198

Speed Bump 201

The Stain 204

Still One of the Brothers 205
Streets 207
Testing Hose 209
Tight Squeeze 211
Train to NYC 212
Training Fire: Too Many Fingers in the Pie 214
We Need to Move Quickly 218
What the Hell Was That!? 220
Where There's Smoke, There's Fire...Sometimes 222
Who Was the Astronaut? 224
Winter 225
The Wood Man 229
Yes, I Have One of Those 230
You Abandon the Pump?! 231
You Need to Pay Attention 233
Yuck! Watch Your Step! 235

My Good Friend—The End 237
Glossary 241

Acknowledgements

To all my former students, classmates, brothers and sisters in the fire service, friends all, who read and enjoyed many of my stories and encouraged me to put them together into a book, I give my sincerest thanks.

To Sue: My partner, assistant, editor, illustrator, critic, wife, and best friend, I can never thank you enough. Without your love, help, and encouragement this work would never have gotten done.

Lew LeBlanc, 1998

Introduction

Having worked in the fire service and fire training for more than thirty years, I guess it's no real surprise that in addition to living the life, I also like to read about it. In my personal library, I have stories of just about every disastrous fire and calamity that has ever happened in modern times. The collection is growing all the time. I also have books about careers, as well as the life and times in the fire service, written by those who lived and worked it.

One of the first books I got many years ago was Dennis Smith's <u>Report from Engine Co. 82</u>, a great work about firefighting in the south Bronx in the late 60s and early 70s. I am fortunate enough to have a copy of <u>Ready to Roll...Ready to Die</u> by retired district chief Paul F. Cook of the Boston fire department, autographed to me by the author. Who can speak of books from the Boston fire department without bringing up the name of Leo D. Stapleton, retired chief and commissioner? I am very fortunate to also have an autographed copy of his first work, <u>Thirty Years on the Line</u>, covering happenings during his long career in the city of Boston. Mr. Stapleton has written many other works as well, and I have several of these in my collection.

I am a lover of nonfiction, so when I shop for reading material, I look carefully for what is available. Fictional stories about fires and the fire service abound. Maybe I'll read them after I finish all the nonfiction stories. Perhaps I'm just looking in the wrong places, but I have not run across stories from the smaller, suburban fire departments. A fire is the same no matter where it burns. Some are bigger...much bigger, but they are still fires. The type of person who takes the job of firefighter is the same anywhere you go. Of course, you have some who just want it said that they are firefighters and love to wear the uniform. You get that element with any group. But the men and women who look for this job, this kind of life because they love it are a unique breed. They live and work together. They socialize together. Everywhere they go they "talk shop." A firefighter from anywhere can walk into a firehouse anywhere else and be greeted as a brother or sister and feel like they're home. They are part of a culture that has to be lived to be truly understood. It's easy to tell fire stories to a group of firefighters. When firefighters tell stories with one another they all speak the same language and use the same jargon.

Once I had retired, I found myself out in the world much more than I had been during my thirty-something years on the job. I had to learn to talk to non-fire people again. I got better at it. Like many people, I started using social media on my computer. I found very many old friends and classmates, many who were not involved in the fire service. I started to write some old memories for friends to read. I wrote these stories so the lay public could understand what was being said: changing jargon, simplifying, and explaining things in more detail.

I called them my "War Stories." Well, I must have done something right because people loved to read them. Some told me that they looked forward to the next one. It was frequently suggested that I should collect these "War Stories" together and publish them as a book. I was getting this positive feedback not only from those in the fire service, like old fire buddies and former students that I had taught in recruit school, but also from many friends from the lay public...regular people!

I thought back over my long career and pulled together a variety of stories that stand out in my memory. Some are funny, some are sad, and some make you just stop and think.

In the interest of privacy, I removed and/or changed the names of people and places. Readers who might not be familiar with the jargon can look and refer to the glossary in the back. These stories are written for fun and are not meant to make anyone look or feel foolish. Although these events happened to me in a suburban town, they could have happened anywhere and to anybody. The result of my work is what you now hold in your hand.

Read, and I hope you enjoy!

The Stories

30 Minutes, Guaranteed

The other day I was thinking about one of those days when nothing seems to go right and it brought to mind this story. Some years ago, I was on duty at station 2 on a Saturday in winter. We were having one of those snowstorms when it snows for a while, then turns to rain, then freezes and turns back to snow.

Well, that morning a young man from south Boston made a fateful decision. He borrowed his parents' car and went to his job, delivering pizzas for Domino's in our town. We're not on the other side of the earth from south Boston, but it was a damn sight further than I would have gone to deliver pizzas. I don't know how his day had started, but at some point in the late morning, he was sent on a delivery to a home on a windy back road. He drove through the snow on roads so unsafe that that no one should be on them. He arrived at the address: a large home, set way back off the road, with a very long driveway that had not yet been plowed.

Well, he started driving up the driveway, but his car got stuck about halfway...right up to the rockers. He was going nowhere. He got out and started walking the fifty or so yards further toward the house to deliver the pizzas, when at some point, he heard a noise behind him. He turned and saw heavy black smoke pouring from his car.

I don't know who made the call to the fire department, but my partner and I were dispatched with engine 2. When we got there, we had to keep engine 2 on the street, as the driveway wasn't passable. I saw the car with black smoke pouring from everywhere. The driver and the residents of the house were all watching from the porch of the house.

I pulled a 1¾" line to the car and started to cool things down. I tried to open the door, but guess what...he had taken the time to lock the door! Well, I hit the corner of the already-blackened window with my Halligan tool. It shattered and flames shot out. Into the window went the nozzle and the fire was knocked down. We had to force the hood up to finish the job. All the while, the kid who drove the car looked on from the porch, with his mouth open. Well, the car, his parents' car, was a total loss, plus it had to be winched out of the driveway. Maybe he should just have called in sick that day. Hope he got a good tip.

There has been a smoke detector compliance law in effect in Massachusetts since the early 70s. Any home being sold has to have a smoke detector inspection by the fire department. You can't pass papers without the certificate that says you have the right number of smokes, they are in the right places, and they all are working. Basically, if your home predates the law, you can get by with battery-powered detectors. If the home has been altered or added on to, you may need to upgrade your detector system to meet the current standard. The law has recently been upgraded to include carbon monoxide (CO) detectors also. The responsibility for the inspection lies with the seller. Many people use real estate companies to sell their property so the inspection is arranged by the realtors.

Though most are very good and well informed on the laws, I have had some experiences with realtors who showed an incredible lack of knowledge for someone doing their job. I've had calls where I was asked if they needed an inspection. I've gone to homes and found only one detector when more were needed, and the one which they did have was in the wrong place. I've had agents call me up in a panic because they're about to close and they don't have the inspection paper. "Can you come right now?!" Then they've gotten mad when I've said I can't right now; I have other duties to take care of. I always tried to be accommodating, but sometimes you just can't do it when they ask.

Out of all the experiences I've had with real estate agents, one stands out and always makes me laugh. I showed up to do an inspection. This involves walking through the house making sure there is a smoke everywhere one is required and testing each one to make sure they are all installed and working. This house was an older one, so battery powered smokes were acceptable. There were several detectors required. When it was time to test them, the agent took from his pocket a package with a 9-volt battery in it. He put the battery in the detector. I pushed the test button and it sounded, as it is supposed to. I went to move to the next detector and the agent took the battery out of the one I had just tested and went to put it in the next detector. I stopped him and told him that each detector had to have its own battery in it and I had to test each one. He became a bit angry with me and tried to argue. I told him to get the batteries into the other detectors and call me for a re-inspection after he had done that. I don't believe for one second that this man didn't understand the law. I think he was trying to make things easier for himself. Oh well, the law is the law. Just do what you're supposed to do.

Afraid of the Uniform

Many years ago, I responded to a medical emergency. A small boy had fallen backwards off a deck. I came on engine 2 from station 2. The ambulance was coming from across town and would be arriving several minutes later.

His mother was holding him, and as I approached, the boy became hysterical and would not even look at me. I told the mother that I understood; He is scared and hurt.

She said, "No, it's your uniform."

Confused, I asked what she meant.

She said it was my uniform. "He thinks that you're a police officer come to take him away because he's been bad!"

To that, I had no reply. Amazing the kind of crap people tell their kids without any forethought whatsoever!

After You!

One morning, when I was working as the duty captain, I was out on the road in car 2 when I heard, over the radio, a neighboring town responding to a gas problem. There had been a backhoe digging in the yard of a home on the far north side of that town. Precautions had been taken to guard against accidentally pulling up underground pipes. However, there was one gas pipe that had not been known about, and the backhoe caught and broke it. The fire department had responded, as always, and the officer had led his company into the home's basement, with gas meters, to check things out. The meters went into alarm, indicating the presence of a dangerous accumulation of gas. The officer immediately withdrew his company from the house. It was a wise decision made by a competent officer. About thirty seconds later, the house exploded.

I had been listening to the radio traffic and decided that I'd better get back to station 1 because there was a good chance of us being dispatched to respond to this call. Soon after I arrived back at the station, sure enough, we got called to cover their headquarters. Two men, plus myself, put on our gear and responded. When we arrived at that firehouse, there was also a ladder company from another town and an engine company from yet another town. Our job was to respond to other calls in that town, should they come in. There were some that we responded to, but it really wasn't very busy.

The crew I had with me was made up of men who had some time on the job, mostly senior men. The ladder company was a mixture of newer and senior people, and the other engine company was made up of younger guys, led by a young lieutenant. None of them looked like they had been on the job too long. I always said that there is enough work in the job without looking for it or inventing it.

After some hours, the dispatcher called my crew to the front. We walked to the dispatch office, closely followed by that crew of young guys from the other engine. When we got up front, the dispatcher said, "Capt., they want another engine up there and you're next."

I said, "OK," and turned around and saw a look of extreme disappointment on the faces of the young lieutenant and his crew. I guess they were expecting to go to another call. Well, I sure didn't want to see this man disappointed, so I said, "Lieutenant, do you want to go out ahead of us?" His face lit up, so I asked the dispatcher if it would be OK.

He smiled and said, "Sure." So the young engine company went to the scene of the explosion.

Good for them, you say? It was nice of me to let them go ahead of me? Well, maybe, but they had to stay there well into the night, spraying water on a trash heap that used to be the house. Meanwhile, my crew got to sit, relax, eat our meals, and after some hours, return to our own quarters. No need to invent work, and there's no substitute for knowledge and experience, and the wisdom that comes with it.

Air Horn

The first new engine we got after I came on the job was engine 4. It replaced an old open cab 1953 Mack pumper. It was the first automatic, the first diesel, and the first with an air horn. With the pull chain hanging from the ceiling, the horn was handy and really moved traffic. It was assigned to station 2.

About 7:30 one Sunday morning, I was at station 1 and preparing to get off duty. There was a call for engine 4. I don't remember what the call was, but when they were returning, the air horn malfunctioned. It sounded and kept on repeating blasts as the engine returned to quarters. This didn't endear us to some of the people in the neighborhood. One person even got into his car and followed the engine back to the station...just to make sure that they were indeed returning. Had they been responding to a call, that would have justified the use of the horn.

After this man got home, he called fire headquarters. I was standing next to the captain when he took the call and I could hear the man yelling and ranting from where I was standing. He wasn't happy at all! Well, the captain apologized, explained that it was a malfunction, and it would be fixed right away. That put the incident to rest, right? Well...no.

A few years later, I went with my family on a Disney World vacation. My wife often jokes that I can't go anywhere without meeting someone that I know. This time was no different. While at one of the parks, I saw a child wearing a shirt with a logo from a school in the town where I worked. I started talking to the parents, and after some pleasantries, I said that I was with the fire department there. Well, guess who the man was. That's right—it was him! While he didn't blame me personally for the horn, I had to sit and listen to his colorful commentary on the incident. How nice it is to find someone from home when on vacation. Not really.

Ambulance Account

Back in the early to mid 70s, as soon as numbers of certified Emergency Medical Technicians (EMTs) were sufficient, many of our surrounding towns, including mine, purchased their first town-owned ambulances. I can't speak for other towns, but in ours, the ambulance was set up to be self-supporting. Any money raised by the department ambulance went into an account to purchase supplies and eventually a new ambulance when one was needed. The fee for emergency transportation to a hospital was very low at first and the town didn't try too hard to collect it. The residents of our town tended, generally speaking, to have insurance which paid the fee most of the time. Over the years, the fee went up with the cost of everything else. Even after the purchase of supplies and new ambulances, the ambulance account had a very substantial surplus of money in it.

Over the years, the cost of living went up and so did taxes. After a while, it got difficult for departments to keep what they had, given their present budgets. Never mind purchasing anything new. One year, as town meeting drew near, there was a very real chance that the fire department was going to have to lay off two firefighters to meet its budget. Naturally, many other departments within the town all wanted something and were having budget problems, too. It was at this time that the large amount of money in the ambulance account came into the public's eye.

The first night of town meeting that year, before things got started, I heard that the deputy fire chief, a town resident, was approached by a school committee member and told that the school department didn't "think much" of the fire department. Then the school committee member asked for the support of the deputy fire chief in helping the school department acquire the ambulance account money for their own department. The deputy chief flatly refused, town meeting started, and the fight over budgets and our ambulance account began. People argued over which department should get to use that money.

After a while, a resident stood up to speak. He said that since the fire department raised the money in the first place, why not let them keep it and save the jobs of two men. This wasn't received too well by the school department, but when it came to a vote, it was decided to use the ambulance account money to save two fire department jobs, and so we were able to keep up our manpower levels.

However, the next year and ever since then, all the money raised by the ambulance goes into the general fund for use any way the town chooses. So much for the ambulance being self-supporting!

Amusement Park

Among the many functions that we provide at the fire department is the giving of directions to the many people who show up hopelessly lost. Often we can help.

We have a road that runs from one end of town to the other. It is designated by a route number on maps, as well as on signs along the road. People make the seemingly obvious assumption that it's all one road. The trouble is that it is really three different roads. In fact, it changes names three times as it passes through town. Even the house numbers start over again with every name change. Imagine the confusion to those who don't know about this!

One of my favorite stories takes place one summer day in the late morning. I was working at station 2 on the south side of town. I was standing in the open bay door, looking around, when a big, full-size car full of people pulled up. There were three large adults and four or five kids. All were sweating in the summer heat. The driver got out, walked over to me, and asked where the amusement park was.

I looked at him funny and asked, "What amusement park?"

Well, at the time there were several parks relatively nearby. One of them had a name that sounded very much like the name of our town. If you are not listening carefully, it might be possible to confuse the two names. The amusement park advertised on TV pretty regularly. I guess he didn't watch, only listened, and he misunderstood what he heard, thinking it was the town's name. So he loaded up the war wagon, got on the turnpike, got off at the exit for our town, and stopped at the old fire department for directions.

Well, what could I do? He needed directions. I pointed at the road out front and told him to follow it through the center of town. I told him to bear right at the fork onto another road, and follow it until he hit the clearly labeled east-west route. Then I told him to head west and drive for about an hour because it wasn't anywhere near our town. The town it is in is 50 miles away.

He looked at me and said, "You're shittin' me, Man! It ain't here?!"

I explained the name difference. He turned, and with an angry look, got in the car. He seemed to explain what was going on as everyone else looked a bit upset, too. They backed out and headed north...in the direction I had sent him. That park closed years ago. I wonder if they made before then!

At Home In Any Firehouse

Firefighting is very much a family affair. Generations have followed fathers and mothers in the fire service. Generally speaking, when families of firefighters come into the firehouse, they feel at home. My own children have developed a "radio ear" and can understand the jargon. When visiting the firehouse, they know what's being said and know when to be quiet to let the firefighters hear the radio talk. Once, in a New York City firehouse, my son turned down an offer by a lieutenant to come and see the trucks, much to the lieutenant's astonishment. I explained that he had grown up in the firehouse and the apparatus wasn't really special to him. The lieutenant seemed to understand.

This general feeling of comfort seems to be somewhat universal, as I found out one day. It was summer and I was working a day shift at station 2. The station is located right on Main Street. The bay doors were open facing Main Street. I looked across the street and saw a young couple and a little boy walking toward the firehouse. They crossed Main Street in front of the station when the little boy suddenly broke loose and began to run toward me—fast. When he got close enough, he jumped up and into my arms. I caught him with a surprised look on my face as the boy smiled at me and started talking. I couldn't understand him. His parents walked up smiling and explained that the little boy's father was a firefighter in Hamburg, Germany. They were in the U.S. to visit some friends. It seems the boy spent a great deal of time in the firehouse with his dad and felt very comfortable there. So, when he looked and saw the firehouse with the engines, and me, in uniform, standing there, the boy felt right at home. We had a brief visit and they went on their way with the little boy waving good-bye. I guess we really *are* all alike, no matter where we come from.

Auto Body Shop

In the early morning hours one winter day, while working at station 1, we were awakened by the alert tone from dispatch for a fire in an auto body shop. We responded with an engine. I seem to remember running a man short that shift, so working that night was my partner, myself, and the captain in car 2.

We arrived first, with the other engine responding from across town. There were flames shooting from a wall vent on one end of the building. There were several big, bay doors in the front of the building, and an office area at the other end of the building with a steel entry door and a large bank of windows next to it. We had to get in and the bay doors were locked. We could have cut through one and gotten in, but there were easier ways. The captain initially told me to take out the bank of windows, but it was not practical as the sash was steel.

I decided to force the door. I had a set of irons with me. I took the Halligan tool and placed the adz into the jam, then asked my partner to hit it a couple of times with the flat head axe. I then pulled up on the Halligan and the door popped open, just as pretty as you please. You sure can't beat the basics for getting things done!

With the door open, my partner and I donned our face pieces, started breathing bottled air, and entered. We had to make our way across the entire building to the other end to get to the fire. It was dark and we had to inch along. We stayed along the bay doors because the windows, though small, gave some light. We got to the other end and saw the fire coming from the far side and the top of the spray booth and shooting out the end vent.

Just as I was getting ready to open the nozzle, there was a crash and we were getting showered with glass. Someone had taken it upon themselves to start breaking the windows in the bay door next to us. It's a good thing we were wearing our protective gear. I guess it was my partner who then opened that big door allowing easier access for others to the fire area while I knocked down the fire. The roof was opened to let out heat and smoke.

After a lengthy overhaul, the fire was out. There was not too much damage because we got to it quickly. Body shops usually contain large amounts of flammable paints and body filler primers and other things and can be a dangerous place to have to work. It was no real problem this time. It's always great when the plan works!

Baby

Many years ago, while I was on a night tour, the tone sounded. The duty shift was sent to a home where a baby had been found unresponsive. The caller, who was a registered nurse, said she was beginning CPR. We knew what we were going to as we left the firehouse.

We got there and I went inside. I saw the lady who called, standing doing CPR on an infant. She stopped and handed the baby to me. I squatted with the baby and did CPR for about a minute. Then I ran out the door, across the lawn, and into the ambulance, keeping CPR going all the way. We placed a CPR board on the stretcher, placed the baby on the board and continued CPR.

The driver got in and headed for the nearest hospital, with me working the patient. Somewhere down the road, we met up with a paramedic team that was coming to help us. They parked and locked their vehicle, got in the back, and the three of us continued work as we made for the hospital. We got police escorts from two towns as we passed through them.

On arrival, I continued to do CPR on our patient as the doctors and nurses worked their hearts out to save this baby, all to no avail. Our patient, a 4-month-old boy, did not survive.

Before we left, the nurses made us sit and have a coffee for a little while. "I've seen the look before. You guys sit and take it easy for a while," the nurse told us. We did, but left when the baby's parents arrived. I had no desire to face them.

We returned to quarters. It turns out that the RN at the house was the baby's godmother. She was looking after her godson while the parents went out for some dinner: their first time out since the birth of their son. She had put the baby to bed, and when she checked on him later, he wasn't breathing. The godmother then made a call for help and started CPR. The captain stayed at the house to help break the news to the parents when they got home. I never envied him that job.

The whole night was a heartbreaker that was quickly buried as deep as possible, as is much of the baggage we pick up along the way as we do our job. It has to be, or we wouldn't be able to function after a while. But this one stayed with me, and still does to this day. Who can say why this one is different. We've all seen death in our job. Sometimes it's amazing how neat and clean it can be, very matter-of-fact, yet always permanent.

I found out that that baby is buried in a cemetery I know well. It is where my own family members are buried. I was told that the baby's family moved to Canada years back. They come down sometimes to visit, but not too often. Whenever I go to visit my Mom, sister, and grandparents at the cemetery, I always stop and visit with that baby boy. At the time of his death, he was about the same age as my oldest son. I will clean the moss and dirt off his stone and just reflect. Sometimes, I even put flowers down, as he never seems to have any.

This is one of the places where I end up when a trip down memory lane goes awry and I take a wrong turn. This one just won't leave me. Well anyway, we gave that little guy the best chance possible. Sometimes things just don't work out very well.

Bad Ass

We had a guy on the fire department who was a kind of big, loud, and in-your-face kind of guy. He was the kind of guy who sometimes liked to grab people, put his arms around them, and squeeze them until they begged him to stop. Nobody liked it when he did that, but the fire department culture, being what it is, nobody went to the officers about it. You handled it on your own. I usually didn't get involved in the antics with this man. I didn't like the yelling and all the noise, so I tried to stay away. I guess it was inevitable that someday I'd get caught up in the middle of things.

Sure enough, one day he started to give me some verbal aggravation. When I tried to walk away, he grabbed me, wrapped his arms around me with me facing him, and he began to squeeze. I'd be damned if I'd yell for him to let me go, so I bit him. Yes, I bit him on the shoulder, not enough to draw blood, but enough that it hurt. He took his arms off of me, called me every name he could think of at the time, and left me alone. He never put his hands on me again. Problem solved.

Barns

Barns, by their very nature, are firetraps. They are usually made of mainly wood and contain things like hay and straw, animal feed, often fuel for farm tools and vehicles, and a host of other things, mostly all highly combustible. Admittedly, I have limited experience with barns. However, I know many people who have fought many a barn fire and the barn was usually lost. Two of the barn fires I have been at stand out in my mind. One was a total loss and the other was a save.

One night, I had been working a few hours for another guy while he was at school. He arrived about 9:30 and I left for home. When I walked into the house, I heard the home receiver broadcasting a box alarm for a fire. I turned and walked back to the car and drove back to station 1. I got to the station and was told it was a large barn and they wanted another engine right away. The deputy chief grabbed me, pulled me toward our 1953 open cab Mack engine, and told me to drive. He got into the passenger seat and there was a man riding on the step.

This engine was built back in the days before power steering and synchromesh for easy shifting. It had no roof. That was just as well, as you sometimes had to stand up to pull on the steering wheel to make a turn. I knew how to drive this truck alright, but I was a little slower than some guys who were brought up driving these vehicles.

I drove up the street and was going to have to make a right turn to get to the fire. As I got nearer, I saw that a police officer from a neighboring town had pulled his cruiser angled across my lane to keep other vehicles from turning there. The officer was in the street signaling me to go around his cruiser. I thought to myself, "You gotta be shittin' me!" as I cut the wheel to the left to swing wide to get around the police car. Then I had to cut the wheel hard right. As I stood up to pull on the wheel, I saw the deputy duck down on the seat next to me and shut his eyes. The guy on the step was ducking, too. I just looked at the wheel and pulled and pulled—hard. Then the engine straightened out and we were through the turn! Beats me how I managed that, but I did, so I downshifted and continued.

At the end of the street there were fire vehicles blocking our way. On our left, there was a large barn, a silo, and two outbuildings, all fully involved in fire. We had to park and leave our engine there because, with an open cab, the radiant heat was really intense. The barn had been full to the rafters with hay bales. It took several days to put it out. They had to use a backhoe to rip apart the barn and spread out the still-burning hay.

I was at another barn fire which was a spectacular save. There were several factors that led to that save. It was fall and the weather was cool. It happened on a Saturday morning at a time when the new day shifts had just arrived for work and were checking their equipment. Also, the surrounding departments were not busy with calls of their own.

This barn was at a well-known farm in a neighboring town. People would go there to get fresh eggs and some meat, or maybe work in the community gardens. Some would just take their kids to see the animals. They had cows, sheep, pigs, chickens, horses: all the usual animals found on a farm.

Over the station radio, we heard their firefighters being dispatched to the barn. Very soon, we were called to cover that town's firehouse, which was a stone's throw from the barn fire. There was a lot of smoke and little flame. That barn had also been recently loaded with new hay. As things got hotter and the smoke got thicker, we were called to the fire. The calls kept going out to other towns for more and more help. I wound up seeing many firefighters that I know yet rarely see and had never seen at a fire. We were all there, from all over the region, working on that barn. We finally, after some hours, managed to get enough of the hay outside to see where it was burning in the middle of the stacks of bales.

Things were done right. We unloaded the barn and wet down the hot spots and managed to save the barn with no structural damage at all, just some floor damage and one small spot where the siding burned through. It was a good save. Most of the big barns in the town where I worked are gone, either burned or knocked down. I think some even fell down due to lack of care and advanced age. There are still some around the area though.

It's quite an experience fighting a barn fire. In the first story, we used a lot of master streams for a couple of days, but we still couldn't save the barn. With the other barn, it was a lot of work, but all worth it. I can say I helped save a barn!

Belt Buckle

When a person pulls a fire alarm box from the street, all the lights in the firehouse come on and the large bell on the wall begins to tap out the box number. The dispatcher reads the number, checks the location of the box, and sends the proper apparatus.

Years ago, before we had civilian dispatchers, the fire department always had a man dispatching on the watch desk, 24 hours a day. The watch for the ten-hour day shifts was divided equally between the three firefighters on duty: three hours and twenty minutes each. The firefighter assigned desk watch second for the day shifts was designated as the watch for both nights. He could go to bed after ten p.m. We had a single large room with four beds for a bunkroom and the desk watchman had to sleep in the bed next to the telephone. It was his job to answer the phone and do all the other duties assigned to the dispatcher.

One shift, when it was my turn to have the watch for the nights, I was sleeping in the bed next to the phone, having a dream that I don't remember. I remember that I kept hearing a soft bell ringing, like the small bell you would ring to call the butler, if you had a butler. It kept on ringing and I opened my eyes. It was then that I realized that all the lights were on, the house bell was ringing loudly and the telephone was ringing next to my ear, lighting up all three emergency lines. Still, I heard the soft bell.

In the next few seconds, I was more awake and I realized that the soft bell I kept hearing was the buckle on the captain's pants as he got dressed. I sat up and answered the phone. People were yelling into the phone, reporting a house on fire with people still in the house. I read the box number and the location and sent the apparatus. There was a house on fire and considerable damage was done. With deep snow, it was difficult to get to the house to search. Luckily, the report of people in the house was mistaken. We wound up sending a couple of our firefighters to the hospital with minor injuries. It was a long night.

Thinking back now, I know what happens when a box is pulled from the street, and with all that noise, I can't help being amazed that what woke me up was jingle of a belt buckle as a man got dressed.

Bottled Water

This one is just to show you all that it's not always fun and games around the firehouse. Having grown up in town, I had always thought that we had very good drinking water. I guess I never noticed that the quality had gone down.

Well, some years back, we got bottled water in the firehouse. I didn't see the need, then or now. Then I heard the "Voices." They spoke to me and said that whenever the bottle was empty when I was there and alone, I should take it down back, fill it up with water from the garden hose, and replace it into the cooler. It was fine with me and no one complained.

This kept up for about 6 months until, as luck would have it, I got caught. A real can of worms was opened then! I was yelled at and threatened with dismemberment (I think) if I did it again.

In a discussion with one man, I said that we had good tap water, to which he responded, "Well, I happen to prefer bottled water."

(I heard the "Voices" again.) "Goes to show what you know. You've been drinking tap water for the last 6 months!" He didn't speak to me for some weeks after. It even went as far as the chief of department, who asked me to stop and not to do it again.

This wasn't done to aggravate or hurt anyone, or to make anyone in particular look foolish. Why did I do it then, you ask? Well, the same reason we do many things: CUZ. Some folks didn't find it too funny. I thought it was pretty funny then...still do.

Brush

Brush fires were fairly common where I worked. There are large wooded areas in town that many people don't know about, so there was potential for some large fires in the woods. There was one area that stands out in my mind above any others. It's an aqueduct that runs through town. I think there have been more fires in and around that aqueduct than any other place in town. It's a long aqueduct but all our fires were in the same general area. There was access via a gate just off of the street and a hydrant right near the entrance. It was positioned just so we really couldn't lay supply hose from it, but had to keep coming back to refill the engine tanks.

I remember one afternoon going to a fire there. For some reason that escapes me, we had three men on the engine. I was riding on the step. We had another young guy riding passenger in the cab and an older man driving. We stopped on top of the aqueduct and there was fire on both sides of us. I jumped off and took the forestry hose that was coiled on the top of the engine. The other two got out and took the booster hose from the reel on the left side behind the cab. I ran uphill, pulling my forestry, and they ran downhill with the hose coming easily off the reel. When I got to the top of the hill and started fighting the fire, I was tired. When I looked downhill, I saw my two partners, with their booster hose, sitting down on a log at the bottom of the hill—resting! It's a good thing they hadn't run uphill. They probably would have collapsed.

Years back, the aqueducts were controlled and maintained by the Metropolitan District Commission (MDC). There wasn't much done to them to keep access clear. We'd drive down it as far as we could, which brought us pretty close to the fires. Then we'd run our hose down, through the trees and into the woods. Those woods were a favorite hangout/partying place for young people. The woods also backed up to an old gravel pit in the next town over, another hangout. We would most often get these fires at night after the parties broke up, so we got them pretty late and often worked there until after dawn. As soon as we'd flow water onto the fire, it would darken down so we couldn't see anything. Then we would have to walk through the woods with our helmets with the face shields down to protect our eyes. Sometimes that wasn't enough.

At one nighttime fire, we knocked the fire down, and while walking through the woods in the pitch dark, the captain, walking just ahead of me, fell into a hole about 8 feet deep. There was a shopping cart and assorted debris on the bottom. The captain injured his back slightly, but he is lucky he didn't break anything.

After some years, the MDC was replaced by the Massachusetts Water Resources Authority (MWRA) who took an interest in those aqueducts. They went right down the middle of the aqueduct cutting the trees down. They took all the brush and trees and piled them high to the sides and intended to pick them up later. Trouble was we got some of our famous brush fires before they did pick it up. We drove down the middle and tried to pull our hose over the brush piles. It was then that we found that the trees and brush were not cut flush with the ground. There were small stumps, about six inches high, sticking up everywhere, and they were sharp. Sure, we learned to watch out after the first fire, but the lesson was learned the hard way.

After a while, things were cleaned up and the fires there became routine. It was worse when the weather was hot and dry. The fire would get burning down below the ground in the peat. You'd think you had it all out, and then we would have to go back a couple of hours later to put out all the hot spots where the fire popped back up again.

Those aqueduct fires continued for most of my career. After I retired, they seemed to stop. I'm not sure why. Maybe someone just had it in for me and wanted to keep me busy. Maybe the evil spirits were playing with me. Either way, those aqueduct fires were a pain.

Buddy Breathers

Our self contained breathing apparatus (SCBA) has changed a lot over the years. I remember the demand units where the air had to be sucked into the mask. If you lost the seal of your mask to your face, the mask would fill with smoke. Now with the positive pressure units, the mask is always pressurized with air. You don't have to suck the air into the mask anymore. However, if you lose that seal, instead of smoke getting into the mask, you'll just blow your air supply away!

The air bottles have gotten smaller and lighter and hold more than the old ones that I started with. The whole SCBA unit is smaller and lighter. However, new things keep getting added to it. There are several different companies that make them, but my favorite story involves breathing equipment that my department uses.

One of the things they added to our SCBAs was a buddy breathing system. This consists of a hose that extends down from the regulator to the wearer's side. On the end of the hose are two couplings, one male and one female. The male coupling had a kind of release on it in the form of a small collar that you pull back to engage or disengage the coupling with its counterpart. When that collar was pulled back, the air would flow freely from the hose. The idea was that if a firefighter were out of air, he could take his buddy breather and attach it to yours, coupling to coupling, and you could share the same tank for as long as you needed...or as long as the air lasted. Great, in theory. Two people breathing the air from only one tank would greatly reduce the amount of time you could get out of that tank. To tell you the truth, I'm not sure I have any "buddies" where my air is concerned. I would use all my air to get you out to a safe place for sure, but I don't really think I'd be inclined to give my air to you. Thank god I never had to make that choice.

When the buddy breathing system was introduced, those couplings were kept together in a kind of pocket on the left side of the frame. But there was a problem with this system in that the couplings on the end of the hose would always fall out of their pocket and they'd be in your way, bouncing around as you felt your way along.

When we finally got some new breathing equipment, they came with the buddy breathers already installed. Shortly after we got it and became familiar with it, as an instructor at the state fire academy and department training officer, I was able to get the use of a trailer from the Massachusetts Firefighting Academy (MFFA) for a long weekend. The trailer had a three level maze in it and was used for training in search and rescue, air consumption drills and a host of other drills involving the

breathing equipment. In it, you would feel your way around in some of the darkest dark you can imagine. You had to squeeze through trap doors between levels and find your way to the exit on the top level.

The evening came for my group to drill in the trailer. Things went well. All the guys got through and were getting used to the new SCBA. Then I took a turn. I did fine for a while. I made it to level two and hit a dead end. I went back and found another way up to level two. As I was going through the trapdoor to level three, my air suddenly started to free flow and I couldn't stop it. I was losing my air supply. I checked for the problem as best I could in the dark but I could find nothing wrong. I took off my SCBA and called for someone to turn on the lights. When they did, the problem became clear. The collar on the male coupling on my buddy breather was stuck back and this allowed all my air to free-flow out. Being a large man, it had been a squeeze for me to get through the hatch opening. What had happened was that as I got through, the coupling was pressed hard against the side of the opening, the collar was pushed back and stuck, and it allowed all my air to escape. This was unacceptable. Thank heaven this was training. This could have been deadly at a real incident.

I went inside and called the chief of department at home and informed him of what had occurred. The next morning we talked and I told him just how it happened. I got off work and went home and the chief called the sales rep for those SCBAs and told him what had happened. The manufacturer was skeptical.

A few days later, they sent someone to investigate. The rep came to the firehouse, and with him there, the chief called me at home via conference call and I told them what had happened. I was told that the rep said that it couldn't happen that way in a million years, or something like that. They went out to the trailer, and lo and behold, they were able to deliberately cause it to happen again, not once but twice! The chief ordered all of the buddy breathing equipment taken off of our SCBAs and the rep went back to the manufacturer to ponder the problem.

The chief told me that the complaint had more credibility coming from me than from others on the department. I was a very senior man: captain, shift commander, training officer, fire academy instructor and support staff member for over twenty years. With all of that, I spent more time wearing these SCBA units than just about anyone. They really had to take my report seriously. The chances of the problem occurring due to my having done something wrong were small.

We used the SCBAs without the buddy breathers for a couple of months. Then one day, when I was on duty, that sales rep came back. The chief called me into the kitchen. The rep had three prototypes of pockets/holsters made up by the manufacturer. He laid them on the table in front of me. They were made of the same material as the SCBA straps, were deep, and had covers that folded over the top. Two fastened with Velcro and one with heavy snaps. Their idea was to better protect the couplings to keep them from falling out and getting in the way. The rep said that since I was the one that had experienced the problem, they wanted my input as to which one was best.

He and the chief left me alone with the three pouches so I could take my time and look them over. I looked at each one. Choosing the best one didn't really take long. One of the holsters stood out. It was sturdy and had a slimmer profile compared to the other two. I thought this one would stand less chance of getting snagged as we crawled around in the dark. Plus, it had a thick cover that fastened with two strong snaps. I called the rep and the chief back in and told them which one I had picked and explained why. The rep, who had never been a firefighter, had only one comment. He pointed to one of the other holsters and said that he thought I would have picked that other one because it closed with Velcro and would be easy to open and close. I explained that, with a gloved hand, opening a pouch would be no problem. Snaps were strong and would stay fastened. Velcro could get snagged on something as we crawled around and would likely open and the couplings would fall out, resulting in the same problem we were trying to eliminate. As for fastening it closed again, I said that if I needed to open it, I wouldn't have to worry about closing it again until I was outside and had plenty of time. This explanation seemed to please him.

Then we had our buddy breathers put back on the units, but *with* the pouches installed. I'm still not sure who might be willing to share their air with a buddy breather, but at least the pouches worked. They stayed secure and didn't fall out. Not a bad solution.

The SCBA company didn't make the incident widely known. Most breathing equipment still does not have the newer holsters, but I've seen some being used by students who come through the academy from time to time. I guess it's an option. I always thought it should be made standard and all old units retrofitted. If some poor soul, somewhere, sometime, suffers this same problem and loses his air in a real fire situation, he'll probably get killed. That would be tragic. The manufacturer knows about the problem and has the solution for it. I guess that's big business for you: profits first. The thing that gets me is they didn't even name the holster after me!

Interesting side note: It seems that the company would like to keep this potential problem out of the public's eye. Sometime after that incident, a man from my department was at a trade show where he went to a booth belonging to that same SCBA company. He saw one of those buddy breather pouches on a unit and asked about it. Of course, he knew the whole story but did not let on. He was told by the man in the booth that it was developed as an option available with the new units. The man from our department said something like, "Really? I thought you made them because a training captain not far from here blew his entire air supply away when the coupling came out and stuck open." Then he walked away from the booth. A little later, he returned to that spot only to find that they were gone. I wonder what motivated them to pack up and close their booth so early.

Burn Permits

There has been a state law against open burning for many years now. There are exceptions to it though: cooking fires with permission, or special purpose fires, like bon fires, for celebrations and possibly a few others exceptions. Other than that, the state allows open burning of brush and garden debris each year from January 15th to May 1st inclusive. The state provides the guidelines and the whole thing is regulated by the local fire departments.

Many cities and densely populated towns do not allow any outdoor burning at all. In the town where I worked, a resident who wanted to burn had to come to the public safety building, fill out a form, and get a copy of rules and regulations. This permit was good for the whole season as long as you followed the rules. The resident only had to call by phone each day they wanted to burn. It was up to the fire department duty officer to say whether or not there will be any burning on a given day. We would not allow burning if, for instance, it were a very windy and dry day. The dispatcher would check with the duty officer each day to find out if burning would be permitted that day.

January 15th in New England is usually pretty cold and often snowy. That seems like a great time to burn without any chance of the fire spreading. Most of the public, however, doesn't seem to agree. They wait until more comfortable days in early spring. Those days are nice, but often dry and the wind picks up. Then, of course, you have the procrastinators who wait until the last minute. Waiting like that sometimes comes back to bite them.

One Sunday, May 1st, I was leaving the house for work. I was to be the duty captain. It had been dry and as I left the house, I noticed that the wind had picked up. It was pretty windy when I got to work. After a while, I went outside to check on the wind again. The wind had picked up even more. I came back in, called down to dispatch and said, "No burning today—too windy."

A few hours later, I got a call from the dispatch office. They said that they were getting calls from residents requesting permission to burn, and when told they couldn't, the people got irate, even nasty. The dispatcher asked if I could take some of those calls. I said, "Sure."

Well, they had an irate lady on the phone at that moment. I told them to send the call up. I answered the phone, "Captain LeBlanc. Can I help you?" The lady wasn't irate or nasty with me, but asked why there was no burning allowed on the last day, and a Sunday to boot. I explained that the responsibility for the safety for the people of the town and their property that day was mine. It was up to me whether or not to allow burning. I thought it was too windy to burn safely. So, on my authority, I decided against allowing burning. I got no argument at all. She thanked me for my time and hung up. She was very nice. I didn't get any more calls from dispatch that day.

I don't know how the rest of their day went, but there was still no burning. Yes, I said, "No burning" on the last possible day, Sunday. I imagine my name was taken in vain by some, perhaps many. I'm sure my fan club didn't get any larger that day either. But it was still too windy to burn!

Burning Books

Years ago, I was on duty at station 1. It was the last day of school for the summer. A boy who lived nearby had gotten home from high school, and I guess he was told he had to mow the lawn. The mower was in a large, two-car garage that was not attached to the house, but stood very close. It was a warm day, but nice, as June often is if it isn't raining!

He opened the garage door, filled the mower with gasoline, and left it in the garage. This was when bad judgment took over. He decided to burn his schoolbooks to celebrate the beginning of summer. He piled them on the driveway, well outside the garage, and he got the gas can and poured some gas on his books. I guess he didn't see the gas he had spilled between the mower and the books, but when he threw a match on the books, the flame shot into the garage, engulfed the mower, then quickly spread.

We got the call for a garage fire. As we turned the corner onto the street, we could see the garage was a huge ball of flame and the fire was extending to the side of the house. We got our water supply, called for more help, and as the outside wall of the house was now burning, our first effort was to put out and protect the house. As we advanced down the driveway behind our hose streams, we heard the sounds of aerosol cans bursting. That made us pause for a minute, unsure of what the noise was.

It was quite a scene, but we had things under control shortly. I noticed that there was a window on the second floor where the fire had scorched the house. It was closed. The gods were smiling on this boy. If this had been *my* house on a day like this, that window would have been open and the fire would have entered the second floor of the house. That would have been a whole different ball game then! But the house sustained some minor exterior damage. The garage was totally destroyed, along with the mower and all the family camping equipment, including two canoes. I guess they were big camping fans. Wonder how they spent *that* summer. It sure started off with a bang. Oh yeah, he never did get the lawn mowed that day.

Canine Arrest

In our line of work, we see some strange things, and if you stay around long enough and you think you've seen and heard it all, just wait. It gets stranger. Back a few years, our new firehouse was being built and we were in temporary quarters in the form of trailers: one for the crew and one for the duty officer as an office. The apparatus was housed in a temporary building. All this was located on the site of the old parking lot of the old building.

At that time, I was an acting captain. I was working an overtime day shift and was in my office doing some paperwork. Around early midday the phone rang. I picked it up and was hit with a loud, rapidly speaking voice. It was a member of the crew at station 2 and they were screaming into the phone at me. I calmed them down as well as I could and from what I was able to gather, there was some kind of emergency at a veterinarian's office down the street from them involving a dog and they were requesting a defibrillator. I couldn't make any sense out of this, but there was a call for help. So I told the crew from station 2 to respond and find out what was going on. I told them *not* to leave that defibrillator there and to be prepared to respond *with* the defibrillator if we received another call. I said that I would be responding also, in the car.

I hung up the phone and called dispatch. I said that engine 2 was responding to the vet's office along with car 2. The dispatcher right away began to lecture me about protocols with the SAED, what I should do, what I couldn't do, and how OEMS would come down on us hard, and so on. I was taken by surprise and getting annoyed. I told the dispatcher that I was in charge and everything there that day belonged to me and he needed to get the apparatus dispatched! I got in the car and left.

When I got to the call, the first thing I saw was my engine crew coming out of the building looking upset. They said the dog had died. Still not making any sense, I went inside to talk to the staff. Well, it seems that a veterinarian had elected to perform open-heart surgery on a staff member's German shepherd, even though they were not properly equipped for this kind of surgery. As luck would have it, something went wrong and the dog went into cardiac arrest. They began open chest cardiac massage and kept it up while trying to decide what to do. Someone remembered that the fire department had defibrillators and they made a call for help by phone. The dispatcher answered the phone, listened to the problem, told them we couldn't help them, and hung up. He did not notify the fire department of the call. This was most certainly beyond the dispatcher's authority.

Well, in desperation, the vet's office sent a staff member to the firehouse down the street. The crew there, being dog lovers, made the frantic call to me. By the time the engine got there, work had been going on too long on the dog and the doctor had declared it deceased.

Now things were making sense. I'm not a dog person. I never had a dog in my life. I don't really dislike them, but never liked them enough to own one. I am not familiar with a dog's physiology. However, I'm quite certain that our semiautomatic defibrillation equipment was designed for and meant for use on humans. They were not adjustable for use on different species. I told that to the veterinarian staff in the most tactful way I could and expressed condolences at the loss of the dog. We cleared and I returned to quarters.

The chief of department stopped by shortly and I informed him of the call and of the dispatcher's mishandling and his attitude. Well, the chief went into orbit and went to the dispatch office. Don't know what he said, but that was the last day I know of that that dispatcher worked.

Well, before the end of the day, the story went completely around the world and everyone knew. I'm not really sure exactly *what* they knew. Rumor circulated that I had ordered the engine crew to respond and assist by defibrillating the dog. This was certainly not the case. I sent help to investigate a vague emergency call. But I guess you have to get used to stories circulating. After all, there are always large numbers of people who weren't even there who claim to know the facts better that you!

Carbon Monoxide

We hear about car accidents, fires, and catastrophes and all the carnage and blood and guts and injuries. Sometimes it's just as neat as you could imagine. One morning, not too far into the shift, we heard the next town over being dispatched to a home for smoke seen coming out of the house. They arrived and saw through the windows a smoke condition inside the house, and I guess they forced entry. Then the captain's voice came on the radio, urgently requesting our ambulance, as well as the ambulance from another town, to respond to the location. He said they had four code blues. "Code blue" is our jargon for an individual in cardiac arrest. We got into our ambulance and off we went. When we arrived, we were told to stand by. Engines and firefighters were there, and two ambulances had already left for the hospitals.

It turned out that, for some reason that will never be known, the family car had been left running in the attached garage overnight. The car had long since run out of gas. The "smoke" condition was really exhaust, visible in the house. When they forced entry, the house was found to be full of car exhaust. The family must have felt that something was wrong. In an upstairs bedroom, the mother was found. Her two daughters were with her, one age five and the other one a couple of years older. The first two ambulances had taken these three patients. I heard that the youngest girl still had a pulse, though I never found out how they made out.

The father was found in his bathrobe on the kitchen floor, just feet from the door to the garage. He must have realized what was wrong and tried to do something about it, but he never made it beyond the kitchen. A doctor had appeared from somewhere and pronounced him deceased, so we didn't have any patient to transport.

We did, however, have to take part in the search of the house for more victims. It's a terrible feeling to search like that. Every time you open a door or look in a closet, you pray to find no one, yet you prepare yourself to work in case you do. Well, we found no one else and, after a while, we were released.

Thinking then and now, I'm just amazed. Death came just as neat and clean as you could want. They might as easily have been asleep—a whole family. It seemed that they realized that something was wrong...but too late. Of course, we'll never know how the car came to be left running and forgotten. It was a hell of a high price to pay for a mistake.

Chop Saw

One summer day when I was working as duty captain, we had the whole shift at station 1 for a drill. During that time, we got a call requesting the ambulance to a home for a carpenter who had cut himself. Calls like this are almost never good. The apparatus all left from station 1, and I, in car 2, was able to get out quickly and arrived at the address well ahead of the others.

I got out of the car with my medical bag and was greeted by a man standing in the front yard, clearly waiting for me. I was thinking that this had a bad feel to it, as I asked the man where the patient was.

He told me it was him. As I looked at him closer, I saw he had a line of small blood spots, almost pinpricks, running top to bottom right down the center of his button-down shirt. Other than that, he didn't seem to have any injuries.

When I inquired as to what had happened, he told me that he had been using a large chop saw. The blade came off when it was running. The blade came at him and sliced off his tool belt, then walked up his breastbone, leaving the row of small pinholes. Then it flew over his shoulder and stuck in the ground behind him. Other than the small injuries to the chest and shattered nerves, there were no other injuries. I couldn't believe what I saw and heard. No lottery tickets or casino trips for this guy. I think he used up all his good luck for some time.

City at a Standstill

The people who take this job, who really want to do the job, are all cut from the same mold. I've heard it said that firefighters are a strange breed. They'll lay down their lives for one another, yet they'll castrate one for another for a lump of sugar. Interesting theory, and not entirely untrue. But it is truly a brotherhood. This is clearly demonstrated when a brother or sister is in danger or killed in the line of duty.

In 1999, there was a terrible fire in a vacant cold storage warehouse in Worcester, Massachusetts. Things went bad when two firefighters were lost in the building and running out of air. The radio traffic between those two men and those outside the building was heartbreaking. A massive search began. Eventually, four of the searchers were also reported missing. After a while, all radio traffic from the missing men ceased. Still, the firefighters from the city of Worcester entered that inferno in search of their brothers.

The chief in command was determined not to lose any more people and had to physically stand in the doorway to keep any more men from entering the building. They set up big lines and guns and fought it from the outside. In the end, six Worcester firefighters were killed in the line of duty. Now the search for their remains had to begin.

Some days later, while the Worcester firefighters were still at the scene in search of their brothers, a memorial service was held in the city. I was one who had the honor to attend. It was a sight to see. Roughly 40,000 uniformed firefighters from around the world attended. We formed up and began a procession to the Worcester Centrum where the service was to be held.

The service was attended by the sitting U.S. president, the vice president, and the two U.S. senators from Massachusetts, as well as dignitaries from the city and the arch bishop of the Catholic Church. As the procession moved through the streets, there was not a sound to be heard, except a drumbeat and the shuffling of thousands of feet on pavement. People everywhere stopped to watch and construction workers doffed their hard hats in honor of our brothers. It was a very moving thing to see.

After the family and friends of our deceased brothers and the Worcester firefighters not engaged in the search took their places inside the Centrum for the service, there was only enough room for roughly half of the remaining firefighters. I was one of the lucky ones to get into the Centrum. The rest watched on one of the several large screens that had been set up. Every state was represented, as well as many other countries, for this memorial. It was an honor to be able to be there. I also lost a friend in that fire. Sometime later, when his remains were found, it was my sad honor to attend his funeral.

The brotherhood displayed during this time was incredible. I'm not sure the public understands it and I'm sure I could never explain it to them. But we all felt that we had to be there and bring a city to a quiet standstill.

Confession Time

I've never had any problem teaching my children about fire safety, how to call for help in an emergency, as well as what is OK to do and what isn't. Working one summer Saturday afternoon at station 2, we got a box alarm. A box alarm can be started in one of two ways. If a person phones and reports a fire emergency and it is determined that it cannot be handled by the on-duty people, the officer can order the dispatcher to "Strike the box." That means the dispatcher can transmit this box alarm through the alarm system to get off-duty people to come back to the firehouse. These firefighters can then get additional apparatus and respond to the fire.

The second way to have a box alarm come in is when someone pulls the hook directly at a pull box on the street. These are usually located on utility poles throughout an area. The engines respond to the location of that particular pull box and decide what help will be needed. Often, when we arrive at these pull boxes, we find nothing. People, usually kids, pull it to see what happens, for fun or whatever.

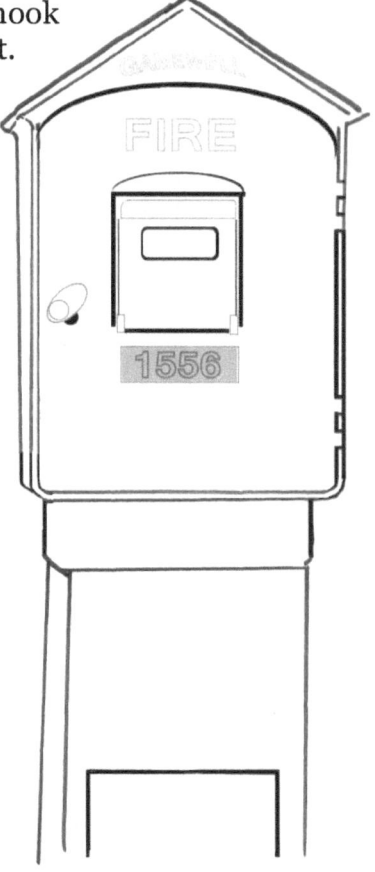

Well, in this instance, the box was pulled from the street. My engine was first due. On arrival there was nothing to be seen, except some younger neighborhood children playing nearby. It was an apparent false alarm, so I told the other responding apparatus to return to quarters. I got out, and wound the internal spring. (Yes, we do still wind them. It's an old system, but it's simple and reliable.) Then I returned to the station and didn't think much more about it.

The next day, Sunday, I was on duty and sitting in the watch room talking to a visitor when a car pulled into the parking area. A man and a young girl (probably around 7 or 8 years old) got out and walked toward the firehouse door. I recognized the man. He was a well-known news anchorman for a Boston television station. It didn't dawn on me at the time, but he lived with his family near where we had received the false alarm the day before. He came into the watch room and said, "Hello," and introduced himself. He introduced the girl as his daughter.

He told me that the girl had something to tell me. She hesitated at first, but her father made her continue. Finally, she confessed that she was the one who tripped the alarm box the day before. She apologized and said she would never do it again.

He asked me to speak to the girl about why she shouldn't do such things. That was an interesting position to be in, one that I was totally unprepared for. I did the best I could, thinking on my feet. I guess it must have been good as the father seemed satisfied.

I've always tried to remember what I said that day in case I was ever in a position like that again, and I was on several other occasions through the years. Having children of my own, I speak the language of children well. With years of teaching and dealing with the public, I've lost any discomfort with public speaking or talking very matter-of-factly with people I don't know. But, I've never forgotten that day when a parent did the right thing.

Cows

The longest road completely contained within the town boundaries is about 2½ miles long. It's a scenic road, and one end is rural-looking and has a herd of cows that grazes in a field and drinks from a pond in that field. On hot days in the summer, the cows cool themselves off by walking into the water in the pond. The traffic has picked up in recent years with hundreds of new condos built on that road. The road is used as a cut-through. Many people who travel this road are not familiar with the habits of farm animals.

One day, a friend came to station 1 to visit while I was on duty. As we talked, a call came in for a cow "stuck" in the pond. Now, this person made the call from a passing car and kept going. This person, most likely, wasn't too tuned in to cows, but probably remembered the cow is not an aquatic mammal, so if it was in the water, it MUST be stuck.

Easy to figure out, you say? No. The captain on duty pulled the hook and sent an engine, ambulance, and two boats to this "cow in the pond" call. I winced as I looked and saw my friend smiling broadly at me. I was sure I'd die a thousand deaths at his hands.

On arrival, there was no cow in the pond. So, no service needed, not that I had any idea what we were going to do anyway. Plus, I had the eerie feeling that the cows were laughing at us as they stared. Ever been laughed at by cattle? It sends your self-esteem into the gutter, as did the laughter of my friend, which continues to this day!

CPR Card

Many years ago, though I worked at the firefighting academy, I wasn't an instructor. I worked in support services: no direct instruction of the students. We set up and ran the equipment and drove the trucks so the instructors could concentrate on the students.

I became an instructor later. There were some instructors who felt this put them a cut above us and they looked down their noses at us. There was one in particular who was about my age with about the same amount of time on his department as I had on mine—quite a few years. This man thought he was much better than the support staff and didn't treat us very well. For example, one day it was very busy at the academy, much was going on. We both were working at the flammable gas firefighting school, he as an instructor and I as water supply officer. At lunch, the cafeteria was bedlam. It was very busy and I was seated at a table full of support staff with one chair open—the only vacant chair in the place. We had 15 minutes to finish and get back to work. I looked up and saw this man standing, holding his tray of food, looking at the chair. Then he smiled and took his tray and stood at the wall to wait for another seat to open up at another table! No sweat with me, but what an asshole.

Well, one day this man appeared at the window at the crib room. This is where the support staff worked out of and equipment was kept. It seemed that this man was a CPR instructor and yearly taught a class for the office staff. He had scheduled his class, and then looked at his current CPR instructor card. Wow, it seemed to have expired! With a class scheduled, he needed an instructor-trainer to renew his instructor card. Well, who do you think the *only* instructor-trainer in the whole academy at that time was? That's right...pick ME! So, this man had to lower himself to ask a fugitive from a colostomy bag, like me, for help. I knew it killed him to do it. I very graciously agreed to help him. I arranged for him to get his new card quickly. I even arranged to have him get his teaching supplies through my agency, all with one phone call. Well, he thanked me and went on his way.

A couple of days later, I handed him his new card. Very nice of me, right? Yes, it was. Plus, there was a personal benefit. For the next two years, every time he looked at his CPR instructor card, it listed my name as the issuing INSTRUCTOR-TRAINER...and I just know that ate at his guts. Gotcha!

Crematorium

Here's one from the "Did You Ever Wonder" department. A firefighter friend of mine told me his department responded to a call at a mortuary for a fire in the crematorium. The way it was told to me, the corpse of a rather large man was to be cremated. It seems that they had the heat turned up too high and wound up with a grease fire. Urban myth...Who can say?

The firefighters had never been inside a crematorium before. When things calmed down, the staff showed them around. They described how the process worked, from the burning of the body to the grinding up of the oversize remains to fit into the urn.

Then the firefighters noticed a container to the side and asked about it. They were told it was the recycle bin. For what, you ask? Why, for all the prosthetic joints, of course! They get recycled to make new ones for other patients.

That story was an eye-opener for me. I'll have to make sure my prosthetic joints go back to the family when I no longer need them. After all, I paid for them and they're mine!

Did We Lose Something?

One winter, some years ago, we were having a major snowstorm. The town's snow-removal crew was having trouble keeping up with the snow and some side streets didn't get plowed right away. We had put some extra people on duty at the fire station for storm coverage so we would have enough manpower, if needed. We got a call for a well-being check east of the center of town. I was sent on the call in an engine and had a call firefighter with me. We got to the street and found about eight inches of snow. The street had not been plowed, but we had our call to answer so down I went. We got to the address, checked with the resident, and found no problem.

This was a dead end street, and as I turned the engine around, it got bogged down and stuck in the snow. Our engine was equipped with On-spot chains, but they wouldn't work in snow this deep. I reported the problem and was told a wrecker would be coming.

As we waited, we listened to radio traffic. As the radio scanned through the channels, it stopped on the police channel. We heard them talking about hose out on the main road. I thought, "OH MY GOD, NO!" We got out, looked in the hose bed of the engine, and found we had no 4-inch hose. Somehow, a coupling at the end of the hose had bounced out. We had laid a thousand feet of 4-inch hose down the street on the way to this well-being check! We stood there, dumbstruck. The call firefighter opened his mouth to say something. I looked at him and said, "SHUT UP AND GET IN THE TRUCK!" Well, the tow truck came and winched us out to the main road and we went back to quarters.

As a side note, the deputy chief had gone out to try to pick up the hose. A car ran over it when he had an armload and almost ripped his arms off. The traffic drove over and ruined two or three hundred feet of brand new 4-inch hose. Plus, the department had to pay the wrecker bill. Needless to say, I didn't get any pats on the back for a job well done!

Didn't Speak All Day

Years ago in the late afternoon on a fall day, I was working a day shift on engine 2 at station 2 when we were dispatched to a medical emergency, an unresponsive female, in a home on our side of town. We were first due. On arrival, I got the medical bag and entered the home through a ground level door, where I was met by an elderly man. I asked where the patient was and he directed me upstairs to a first floor living room. There, I saw an elderly woman seated in a chair in front of a television, with her feet up on a hassock and a small blanket over her legs. She might have been watching television. I approached and spoke to her but got no reply. Getting closer, I touched her face, then checked for a pulse in her neck. Not only was there no pulse, but she was cold and hard. She had been gone for a number of hours.

When faced with a situation like this, there is really nothing we can do. The patient had been gone too long, and with rigor mortis starting to set in, CPR is not possible. I went back down the stairs and asked the man how long she had been there. He replied, "All day." They were husband and wife and it seems that they had some sort of argument in the morning. She went upstairs to watch television and he went off to do something else. They stayed apart all day and never spoke.

As evening came, he had prepared dinner and went to call her to eat and found her as we did. These two people will never again have the chance to work out a problem or disagreement, or even talk. The end can come very suddenly, and it did. Some have told me that there are often lessons to be learned from these stories. There must be something useful here that we can walk away with.

Dispatch

When I first came on the fire department, the firefighters had been doing their own dispatching for many years. When you called the seven digit emergency number, the phone rang in the firehouse and was answered by a firefighter who then sent the appropriate response. Except for the officers, we all had to do watch desk/dispatch duty. We followed a schedule so that everyone worked as the dispatcher an equal amount of time, both day and night. That wasn't so bad really. You had to sit at the watch desk, but at night, if it was quiet, you could go to bed at a designated bedtime. The deskman had to sleep in the bed next to the phone. If a call came in, it was his job to shake off the sleep, answer the three emergency lines, and get the proper help on the way. It worked out well because when the phone is answered by a firefighter, that is someone who knows the town and knows what to send without having to reference things first. We often even knew the location of a specific house without having to look it up.

Sometime in the 80s, the town built a joint communication center for fire and police which was staffed by civilians. That system eventually evolved into our 911 dispatch center. Prior to 911, we still had the seven-digit number to dial. After a while, the system started to work pretty well, but at the beginning, some of the original people hired to dispatch left much to be desired. Many were town residents with no public safety experience. Some had police experience only.

There was one summer evening when the fire department was very busy. While off at a call, the dispatcher radioed to let them know that when they were finished there, he had another call "pending." Depending on the call, the police can, and often do, have pending calls. This is almost never the case with the fire department. The captain asked the dispatcher what the "pending" call was, and was told that it was a report of a garage fire on the other end of town. The captain gave the appropriate orders and both calls were handled and nothing left "pending." The dispatcher was told that the fire department does not keep some calls "pending."

One of my favorite stories involves a well-meaning but misguided dispatcher. She was an older lady with little or no public safety experience and minimal training. She lived near a large pond. In the summer, the local teens and other young people used to hang out near the pond in the evenings. Often there were a great many people there and sometimes there were problems.

One evening, the phone rang in the dispatch center. This lady answered and took the report of a stabbing down by the pond. Proper action should have been to send the police and the ambulance, as well as the engine company from station 2. Well, since this woman lived in the area, she knew the people and the neighborhood. She started to call people she knew in the neighborhood to try and get the victim a ride to the hospital. Imagine, someone who had been stabbed and was bleeding, and the dispatcher was making calls to neighbors to get him a ride!

She never got any of the neighbors to help and by the time somebody in authority found out what was going on and got the proper help on the way, someone else had already scooped the patient up and driven them to the hospital. I don't remember anything about any investigation, although I'm sure there was one. I know the dispatcher wasn't working there anymore after that. Besides the obvious concerns for the patient, it was some pretty bad publicity. Thank heaven things have vastly improved since those days.

Down Vest

Working in the town where you grew up can have its down side. Sooner or later you are bound to see someone you know in a bad situation. You have to separate yourself from things and do your job. Likewise, calls can have their ups and downs and even lighter moments. Anyone who has been in the business for a while will remember Military Anti Shock Trousers (MAST). This was invented by the military as a means to prevent the onset of shock on battlefield wounded till they were gotten to a surgical hospital. They were laid out flat around a patient's legs and abdomen and wrapped around and fastened with Velcro then inflated. There were three sections, each leg and the abdominal section, with a gauge on each to tell the pressure. The idea was to keep the blood flowing to the brain and major organs and not so much to the extremities. Those trousers were all the rage for a while and were considered an advanced skill when we got them in the fire service. We had them in our ambulance and for a time I was the only one certified to use them.

In the mid 80s, we had a major storm in November with a lot of snow, sleet, and freezing rain. That day I had given a talk to the group during a training session about the use of MAST. On the same day, a man who had the day off from work had gone for some drinks at a local bar. He was smart about it and walked instead of driving. Late afternoon on his way home on foot, he slipped crossing the street in heavy traffic and was struck by a car. It happened around the corner from station 2 and I and my partner responded with the engine and were there in about 30 seconds. We found him lying in the street, partly in a snow bank, unconscious and unresponsive. Pulses were present and we started to get what vitals we could until the ambulance arrived. Traffic was terrible and the police tried to control it, but it was a mess. The ambulance came and we were working fast trying to get the patient packaged for movement. A police officer demanded that I get the patient's wallet for ID. I looked up at him and flames shot out of my eyes. The officer backed down and said, "When you get a chance."

Paramedics arrived and we got the patient into the ambulance. A medic asked if we had MAST. I answered, "Yes," and then he told us to apply them. We had to cut the clothing off. It was cold and wet and we had the heat blowers at full blast. As we cut the clothes, we cut through a down vest and there was a <POOF> and an explosion of feathers everywhere. Oh well, we kept working. MAST went on and were inflated, IVs started, and transport done. The patient remained in the same condition. More things were done in the ER and a helicopter called for transport to a trauma center. The patient died in the helicopter on the way.

I found out the next day that this had been a man I had known all my life. I had gone through school with him all the way, though he was a year behind me. Seeing him out of context, I didn't recognize him.

We got a nice letter of commendation from the medics and the ER for our skill in using the MAST pants. MAST has gone by the wayside since better things have been developed and they are not in use any longer. That police officer never did get that wallet. He's since retired. I hope he's not still waiting.

Oh yeah, we were cleaning feathers out of that ambulance till the day we got a new one.

The Dragon Escapes

I was on duty at station 1 late one afternoon around the winter holiday season. We got a call for a fire in a house. The address was in an area where hundreds of condos had been built. The call came from one of those condos, and like all the others, it had a fireplace. Though the lady of the house knew next to nothing about fireplaces, she decided to build a fire for atmosphere and to take the chill off.

It was a large fireplace so naturally the lady assumed it could hold a lot, so she decided to fill it—to the top. She put in logs and shingles along with paper and assorted other kindling. Then she lit the fire. Maybe she knew a bit about the building and lighting of fires, or maybe luck intervened, but it did indeed light.

The fire took off and before the lady knew it, smoke was filling the condo, quickly followed by flame. The fire shot out the front of the fireplace and up to the ceiling, where it mushroomed out in all directions. The fire traveled across the room and set fire to her Hanukah decorations on the other side of the room. Then it started to spread.

Somewhere during the time that the fire was leaving the fireplace, the lady panicked and ran to call the fire department. If the lighting of the fire involved bad luck, the luck changed direction when she called for help. The fire department was pretty close and there was no traffic. Help got there fast. We were able to extinguish the fire rather quickly with only moderate damage.

The lady of the house was in tears as she explained what had transpired. When asked if the flue was open, she asked, "What's that?" We explained what the flue was and how it has to be opened up to allow the smoke, heat, and fire to be drawn up and out of the chimney. We went to show her the control only to find that it was the kind located up inside the fireplace. After the fire was lit, she couldn't have opened it even if she had known about it.

The full spectrum of luck, both good and bad, was with that lady that day. She could have burned herself out of a home, possibly taking her neighbors' homes with it. Fortunately, it didn't work out that way.

The moral of the story? Don't play with things you know nothing about; Ask before you touch; Bigger isn't always better; Everything isn't always as it seems. I think I could keep going. The moral of this story covers a lot of ground!

Drive from Maine

The human thought process is a very interesting thing to explore. It gets us through the day and through some very trying times. It's worth looking at the thought process in an emergency situation. It's incredible what it makes some people do. This is the process that makes some go back into a burning nightclub because they have to get their coat, reenter their burning home to retrieve some "important" item, or stand in the surf during a hurricane. The list goes on. Well, I never had a burning nightclub to deal with, but even my memories abound with foolish things people have done. Sometimes it catches up with them.

Many years ago, before paramedics, the EMS system was made up of basic EMTs. We knew a great deal, but our help could only go so far. Back during a time when the department was trying to cut overtime expenditures, I was working with the shift officer at station 2. We were getting off duty at 6:00 p.m. Shortly before that, we got a call for chest pain at a doctor's office in the center of town.

The officer knew the night shift would be in soon to man the engine, so he took me in car 2 and off we went. It turns out that a rather elderly resident had been in Maine with his wife when he began having chest pain that got progressively worse. His wife, not knowing what else to do, put him in the car and began driving back to town...to the man's doctor's office. They made it back. The man walked into his doctor's office, lay down on the examining table, and went into cardiac arrest.

We were called. When I got there with the officer, the ambulance was there with the crew inside doing CPR on the patient. The stretcher had not been brought in, as there was no room for it. This was the smallest space for a medical office that I've ever seen. I jumped in to help and we did a few rounds of CPR, and when we were ready, we picked up the patient bodily. It was then that we noticed the wires. The doctor had hooked him up to a 12-lead EKG and never told us. Back down went the patient while we disconnected the wires and picked him up again. There was hardly enough room for us to pass, and going around corners was tough. Outside the back door, the officer and the police had set up the stretcher. We had to hand the patient over a railing to get him all the way out and get him onto the stretcher. We were spent by now, just working to get him outside. CPR was performed all the way to the hospital and they continued it in the ER, but to no avail. The patient expired.

Working as I did in the emergency services, in my mind certain logical actions should be taken. It's hard to empathize with many people and the actions they take. It all seems black and white to me and anything else just seems stupid. What would she have done if he had gone into cardiac arrest on the highway on the way back? I wonder how things would have turned out if she'd taken him to a hospital nearby in Maine. We'll never know.

Drowning

In our area, we have a large lake that extends into several towns. We have our town beach and a lot of other shoreline, and it all comes with its inherent problems. But a neighboring town has the state park and the beach that goes with it. It's just down the street from an exit on a major highway. As soon as the weather gets hot, it's a major draw, with a large number of people coming from the city of Boston. They come in droves on the weekends for a day in the country, swimming, and picnicking. Weekends can be a nightmare. Sometimes, the weekdays can be bad, too.

Late on a hot weekday morning, I was on engine 2 from station 2 returning from a call. Our ambulance was transporting. The town that has the state park in it was busy at a call, so we, being the closest crew available from anywhere, were sent to the state park beach for a reported drowning.

We got there and found that we couldn't get the engine right up close, so we got our equipment and ran for the beach. We found CPR in progress by a lifeguard and a bystander at the water's edge. They stopped as we approached, but I told them to continue while we got our tools ready. Then we took over with me at the head, responsible for breathing and airway management with a BVM, and my partner doing chest compressions. No defibrillator was used due to the water that was everywhere.

Our patient was a 12-year-old girl on a day trip with a group from the city. As I inserted an airway, I asked what happened. They said someone had stepped on her in about six feet of water. She was unconscious, lying on the bottom. The lifeguard had pulled her out with help from bystanders and began CPR. I asked if anyone had reported her missing and was told that no one had. We had no idea who she was.

This was not one of those neat, clean calls. Drowning is a very tough, messy thing to deal with. We kept up CPR and kept her mouth and airway clear until an engine company from another town arrived with a paramedic ambulance. There was work for all. We worked fast and soon we were ready to load.

"OK, Everybody ready? OK, 1-2-3-4-5-GO!" We picked up the stretcher and ran for the ambulance, loaded her up and they were off for the hospital. The best job possible was done by those professionals on scene. Unfortunately, she did not survive. Well, there were lawsuits and finger pointing.

This was very typical of the problems we have in and around the lake each year as the weather warms. What is the point of this tale, you ask? I would have to say the seemingly total disregard for the children that we see. Who is she? We don't know. Did anyone miss her? No, no one missed her. No one saw her go under. I don't know if her parents were there, but what about those responsible for the welfare of those kids in their care for the day? It just boggles the mind...after we clean up the mess.

Eight Inches of Cold Steel

I was once asked by a fellow firefighter when the town was engaged in the search for a new chief, "So, what would *you* like to see in a new chief?"

Not really seeing anything special about any of the candidates, I answered, "About 8 inches of cold steel."

Funny, I was never asked again. What the hell. If you don't want to know, don't ask!

Eternal Thanks to Those Cops

Just about everyone on the fire department has another job. Some guys do the "Mr. Mom" because their wives have a really good job. We all supplement our incomes somehow. Plus, the days off between our shifts are lumped together making a second job possible.

I've done many different things on my days off. One of them was working for a private ambulance service. It was good work and I learned a lot, much that could be applied to the firefighter job also. My usual partner was a firefighter from a neighboring town. He was also trying to make some extra money and worked the same schedule that I did. So they paired us up and we became great friends and had a good time during our days together. We were both relatively sharp and knew this job well, but once in a while we made a mistake. The job was really routine transport work, not life-threatening emergencies, but rather a patient needing to be transported to a different location via ambulance. I didn't care about it not being exciting as I got all the emergency work I wanted at the firehouse.

One day, we were sent to Children's Hospital in Boston to pick up a medical team. Then we were to drive to one of the big hospitals in Lowell. There was a child there that needed to be taken back to Children's Hospital. The patient was an 18-month-old boy who, up to that point, had been perfectly normal. That morning he had been sitting on the floor at home, quietly playing, when he suddenly fell to the floor and began to seize. There was just one seizure after another, nonstop. The child had been taken to the hospital in Lowell where it was decided to do the transfer to Children's. On top of that, they had to give him so much medication to stop the seizures that he stopped breathing on his own. He was on a respirator in the hospital, but we were going to have to breathe for him with a BVM with supplemental oxygen all the way back to Boston.

We got to the Lowell Hospital and the medical team went in. It was customary for this team from Children's Hospital to examine and evaluate the patient before transport. They went in and my partner and I walked down a hall through a gauntlet of people, all looking at us. They were the boy's family, all of them, and they knew who we were and were watching us closely. I was worried. I was the driver that day and really didn't know Lowell very well. In the past, any time I had been in that city and asked for directions, what I would hear was always confusing, and every direction involved going over the river. It seemed that the river was everywhere. Getting lost was not an option. I knew we couldn't mess this up.

While the medical team was evaluating the patient, I went to the emergency room, where I saw a Lowell police officer. I explained my problem in detail. When I was done, he said that he'd take care of things. I didn't know what he had planned, but I felt relieved.

When we were ready, we took the patient outside on the stretcher, with my partner bagging the patient to keep oxygen going into his lungs. Into the ambulance everybody went. I got in to drive and the police officer signaled me from his car to follow him. There were three police cruisers leading us. We used our lights and siren, and as soon as we approached a major intersection, police standing by would already have the traffic stopped and the intersection cleared. As we came to smaller intersections, one of the three cars leading me would pull ahead and stop traffic for us, then fall right back behind us. They did this all the way to the highway. From the highway on-ramp I knew my way. I waved my thanks to the officers and got on the highway.

A little preplanning went a long way that day. Those police officers went the extra mile to help. I never knew how the little boy turned out, but we sure owe a large debt of thanks to those officers who gave us the help we desperately needed.

Expensive Phone Call

One evening, I was taking a patient in the fire ambulance to one of our more distant hospitals. I had my lights and siren going. The woman driving the car in front of me just wouldn't pull over and stop like she was supposed to. I could see that she was talking on the phone. She moved over a little bit, but with her going 40 miles an hour and traffic coming toward me, I couldn't get by her car. No matter what I did or how much noise I made, she would not stop. When I finally saw my chance, I picked up speed and got past her. The police cruiser that was behind me then turned on his lights. She must have stopped for him.

A while later, that cop stopped by the firehouse. He told me that he hoped it was an important phone call because he wrote her a hundred dollar ticket for failure to yield. Hope that call was important! What a moron.

Faith in the Guys

Groups of people working together toward a common goal always perform better and more efficiently when members of the group have faith in one another. This is especially true of a fire company. The men and women on the companies place their lives in the hands of each other and take the lives of the other members in their hands. They have to have faith in their partners on the company to do what they have been trained to do. Of course, there are sometimes weak links in the chain, perhaps a new person who hasn't proven themselves yet. Sometimes there are people who are not quite up to the level where they should be. It's the same with every group, but usually those weak links are few and far between. This faith is very important to an officer who has to give orders and know that they will be carried out properly.

On my fire department, faith in the firefighters by the officers was not always shown. I'm not sure of the reasons. It could be self-importance, fear of taking the chance on someone else's word, micromanaging, or perhaps outright lack of trust. In my time on the job, I have seen all of these. When I was promoted and had to command others, I had some firefighters in which I had little faith to make the right decisions. There were others whose word was as good as gold to me.

Some years ago while on a 24-hour shift, I was a lieutenant working at station 2. The captain commanding the shift that day went home sick just after noon. The policy in our department was to run one man short and only call in overtime coverage if a second man is out. Because the captain was the only man out, I, as the remaining officer, went to headquarters to work the rest of the shift in car 2 in command of the shift. A private went from headquarters to fill the empty spot at station 2.

The other man at station 2 was a newer guy, so they went out for street familiarization/driver-training with their engine in their district. I was at headquarters when the alert tone went off and reported a house fire on the south side of town.

I pulled on my gear and left in car 2 as the company from headquarters was preparing to respond. Because the south side engine company was already on the road, they got to the location very quickly. I was about halfway to the call when a firefighter in engine 2 radioed a report of a "working fire." The man who made that report was one of the people that I had absolute faith in. If he said "working fire," then that was good enough for me. I got on the radio to dispatch and ordered the box struck and the tone put out calling all off duty firefighters back to duty. We were going to need the extra manpower.

Striking the box can be an expensive thing to do if there were no fire. Every firefighter who returns is guaranteed a minimum of four hours overtime pay. I've worked for many officers who would have waited until they got to the scene before making the decision to strike the box. I had faith in my men and that day it paid off.

When I arrived, the crew from engine 2 already had a hose inside the building and was searching for the fire. The next engine arrived right behind me and established a water supply from a hydrant. Another engine showed up with firefighters who had answered the recall. I ordered a second line inside and a crew with tools to assist in finding the fire.

It was hard to find the fire. As the smoke got thicker and more manpower was needed, I ordered a second then a third alarm to be struck, calling in fire companies from other towns. It was a long afternoon but we finally located the fire in a crawl space under the living room. None of us would have ever guessed that there was such a crawl space in that house. You really never know what is in people's houses. There was substantial damage but we were able to save the house.

The men and women who responded did a good job. Firefighting is very time-sensitive. I have to think that the few minutes gained by ordering a general recall when I did, upon hearing the firefighter identify it as a working fire and not waiting until I personally arrived on the scene, enabled us to get more firefighters to the fire sooner and probably enabled us to save the home. A little faith in your people can go a long way.

Falling Asleep on the Throne

In our town, we had two nursing homes and two elderly housing complexes. More facilities for elderly housing and care are being built all the time. In one of the housing complexes there lived a very nice, elderly man. He was always smiling, very friendly, and a pleasure to talk to. He was quite large, about 400 lbs., and also had narcolepsy, or at least it seemed that way; He could fall asleep anywhere.

One day, while sitting on the throne in his apartment, he fell asleep. We don't know how long he had been sitting there, but at some point he moved, teetered, and fell forward. As he fell, he caught his credentials under the seat, and as 400 lbs. fell forward off the throne to the floor, certain parts of his anatomy were forcibly removed from his person. I wasn't there for this call, but heard the story from those who were. I never saw this elderly man again. I still cringe when I think of that!

Father's Day

Some years ago, I took an overtime day shift as the captain of the group. It was a Sunday and also happened to be Father's Day. About early mid-morning, I was on the apparatus floor with the bay door open, and I saw a familiar vehicle pass by and turn into our parking lot. I recognized the driver as the wife of the lieutenant on duty. Trouble was, he was working at the other station. I was going to go out and tell her where her husband was, when I saw another car pull in with the wife of another on-duty man. Suspicions aroused, I went upstairs and called station 2 and told the lieutenant his wife was here and to start over; something was going on. Before another few minutes passed, the door opened and the families of all of us on duty came in with bags filled with food. They went into the kitchen and started cooking. They cooked all kinds of breakfast/brunch food—more than we could eat. We had a wonderful Father's Day brunch with our families there at the station.

It seems that this plot had been hatched some days before. When they found out that I was working the overtime, they called my wife to help and enjoy. It was great having our wives and kids at the station for our little surprise celebration, and as the Great Spirit was watching over us, we had no calls during that couple of hours while we enjoyed our brunch. Hats off to the ladies! This was one of the nicest days ever spent at the old fire department.

Fire from Hell

This is the story of what I call the "Fire from Hell," not because of death and destruction, but because things went wrong that shouldn't have. We know that shit happens through no one's fault, and also because of attitude and stupid mistakes. This is a nice mix of the two.

Over the years, our job has expanded to include well-being checks. This consists of a full medical response to an address where someone can't get in touch with or hasn't heard from a friend or relative. Usually, everything is OK, but sometimes not. We were responding to a well-being check with an engine and the ambulance, when a call came in for a house fire on the other side of town. I was in engine 2 from station 2 with the lieutenant. The shift officer diverted us with the engine to the fire call and kept the ambulance on the well-being check. A mutual aid request for an engine to the fire from the next town should have been made. That crew could have been there first. This was not done. This meant another couple of minutes were lost before fire attack. As fire doubles in size every minute, time is a major factor in our business.

Police at the fire scene were reporting fire showing. As we arrived in the engine, the officer radioed for us to remember the recently adopted "Two-in, two-out" policy. We were ordered not to enter until a second company arrived, yet none was en route at the time. This was a misunderstanding of the policy. Entry into the building should have been allowed, but not into the actual fire room. This would have still allowed fire attack. The door at the top of the driveway was a straight entry into the basement. The fire had started in a microwave oven in a closet in the partly finished basement playroom. The fire came out of the closet, climbed the concrete wall toward the unfinished ceiling, into the wall, upstairs, and vented out the basement window.

Since we had been ordered not to enter, I took a line around the side to the window to try and knock down the fire from there. After a long wait for water which never came, I went back around the house and saw my partner, the pump operator, backing the engine out of the now-destroyed garage. It seems that the operator moved the air valve to engage the pump much too fast and engaged the transmission instead. He then realized the attack line had no water. His answer was to keep throttling up. The truck over-rode the maxi brake and lurched forward into the center post between the garage doors. It collapsed the garage and destroyed the cab on our new, first-line engine.

This was a very senior man who should have known better and should have been able to troubleshoot the water issue easily. I reached into what was left of the cab, took the engine out of *PUMP* and reengaged it—s l o w l y. Water problem solved.

The officer arrived with another piece of apparatus and crew. The attack line went to the door. Entry was made and the fire in that room was quickly put out. Too bad by this time the fire was in the wall and up to the first floor.

The second vehicle laid a 4-inch line from the hydrant to the original pump and parked. It parked on a hill with chock blocks in place, but it was winter and water was flowing and ice was everywhere. The truck slid backwards on the ice, down the driveway, caught the 4-inch hose and tore it out of the first pump. The hose flew across the driveway, hit a firefighter in the chest, and knocked him down. He went to the hospital. No serious injury though.

The sudden loss of water to the attack lines when the hose was torn away forced us to withdraw from the house until we got a new water supply. This was accomplished by an out-of-town engine. They caught a hydrant and laid in.

In their haste, the person at the hydrant opened it too soon, filling the 4-inch hose with water. Unfortunately, that hose had not been disconnected yet and was still in the storage bed on the engine. Somehow, that mess was straightened out, water was supplied, and the fire was put out. There was much damage to the house, which, as I hear it, was demolished and a new one built on the site.

That's the end of the story, as I know it. At this "Fire from Hell," there was

- needless fire extension at one end of the house,

- a garage collapse at the other,
- a new fire engine demolished,
- a hose damaged,
- a man sent to the hospital,
- and a load of large diameter hose charged in the hose bed of an engine.

Some of these things wouldn't have happened if training and understanding and attitude were what they should have been. I like to think that things have improved since then. I hope they have. I hope lessons were learned from this fiasco. Sometimes shit happens, but it should never happen because people don't know what they're doing or don't care.

Fireball

Most of us on the fire department have another job we work on our days off. Many involve a job the firefighter had been working in before their appointment to the fire department. I've worked many other jobs, but I found a home at the state firefighting academy, teaching what I know best. There are a good many of us that work there. There are other reasons besides the money, which isn't fantastic. It keeps us sharp on our fire department related skills and lets us in on new skills, tactics, and techniques. We teach many different things there.

One day, I was working at the flammable gas firefighting school. We use real product there—propane and liquefied natural gas. We set fire to it and teach techniques to put it out. You can use hose streams to control vapors, but the fires do not go out with water, and in some cases, water makes the fire get bigger. It's all extinguisher work. This class was a group of employees from gas companies from along the east coast. We dress them up in protective clothing and we use large wheeled extinguishers. We have to supervise closely, as even though these people know about the gas, they are not firefighters.

We were using a prop that simulated a gas leak where two pipes came together. When the gas began to "leak," it was ignited with a torch. (It's important not to let the gas vapor spread around creating a hazardous environment.) My crew went in, but could not put the fire out. We went in a second time with the same result. A third attack was made, this time by two crews and two wheeled units. This is where it gets interesting and shows that even when everything is done properly, things can go bad. We made our attack and put the fire out. Here, several things happened in the span of a few seconds:

- The fire went out.
- The man responsible for lighting the fire put his torch into the vapor to relight it.
- The gas reignited.
- My extinguisher ran out of powder.

- The other crew withdrew.
- A fireball came at my crew.

Without a working extinguisher, we couldn't do anything but quickly withdraw. I started out, then noticed that my crew hadn't followed. I turned and saw them with the fireball wrapping around them. Remember, these people are not firefighters, so I went back in and grabbed them and led them out. I ended up with some minor burns on my lower face.

We all came out OK, but I guess things looked dramatic from the outside. The EMS officer started thinking about casualties. Hose lines were brought into play to cover us. The safety officer jokingly said that there was a boom and a fireball and I had disappeared. He said he was wondering how he was going to write this up. Everything went as it should have, no mistakes were made, yet there was still potential for severe injuries. This speaks volumes about the job of firefighting. It is dangerous all the time, even in training. But, we did adhere to one basic principle that we always stress: We were geared up. We wore everything we were supposed to and wore it properly. That was probably the one major reason that no one was hurt. I often tell my recruits that your gear cannot protect you if you don't wear it all, properly, all the time. Guess we proved it that day—and I still refer to that day as "The day the ignition officer tried to kill me!"

First CPR

When I first became a member of the fire department, I was what they call a "call firefighter." I didn't work any shifts at the firehouse; I only worked when I was called in for fires or station coverage, etc. Back then, there were no paramedics around. Today you can't throw a rock without hitting one—but not then.

We ran the ambulance with basic Emergency Medical Technicians (EMTs), and not everyone was one of those either. The whole EMT thing was new and not all the older guys were into it. To even get into an EMT course, you had to have an affiliation with an emergency service. Well, with my affiliation as a call firefighter, I got into a course, did well, and got my certificate. I was one of only three or four EMTs on the call department.

On Easter Sunday that year, it was a beautiful day. I was sitting on my front lawn when an engine rolled past my house and came to a stop at a neighbor's house a few doors down. The crew got out and went inside. I decided to walk over to see if I could help, not knowing what was going on. I walked in to find my neighbor lying on the floor and the two firefighters kneeling next to him and beginning CPR. They seemed to be having a tough time remembering how to do it. Remember, this whole thing was a new concept then. Being just out of school and with CPR fresh on my mind, I was invited to help. I dove right in, working on a man that I had known all my life.

The ambulance arrived and the patient was loaded into it. I was told to get in the back and continue CPR with another firefighter. We worked all the way to the hospital, but as was so often the case, the patient had been down too long and we couldn't save him.

This was my first ambulance call ever—a full cardiac arrest and on a person that I knew well. Tough way to break in, but I found that I was able to work without getting emotionally involved and look objectively at the call afterwards. While not liking what had happened, I was not bothered by the scene I was just involved in. I knew then that I could handle the job, but my education was just beginning. This was the first of very many calls with the ambulance dealing with almost anything you can think of. I was always able to look at each call the same as I had the first one. While I may not have liked the call, I always did what needed to be done.

Floods

Among the many other things we had to contend with, flooding added a new sense of adventure to the job. It usually happened in the spring, most often after a snowy winter. We often get some heavy rain that time of year. Rain, mixed with melting snow, made for a mess in many parts of town. There would be water in the public safety building and the town and the town center would be under water and impassable.

I remember walking through three feet of water on *top* of a bridge over the river that flowed the length of our town, so we could look over the side of the bridge to check the stick gauge that measured the water's height. When the river would come up, one particular neighborhood near the river would become an island. One of the roads there even has the word "Island" in its name. It is a typical, backcountry New England road that kind of meanders through the countryside. Part of this road and a couple of side streets are at a higher elevation, with I'm told, about 200 houses. When the river was high, the road would become completely submerged and was impassable on both sides of the high spot. Before the water got too high, we'd bring an engine to this area and staff it 24 hours a day, in case anything happened out there. Everyone, residents and firefighters alike, would need transportation to and from the island. In the old days, we used the boats that the fire department had. Later, we would use the 2½-ton trucks provided by the National Guard. They had more room, were faster, and had the ground clearance to make it through the water.

"Island duty" wasn't too bad. Mostly nothing really happened. At first, there was a family that let us use the basement living area of their home as a base. We didn't want to keep imposing, so one of the firefighters would tow his travel trailer out there before the water got too deep and we used that. We'd stay there until the river came down enough for cars to pass through the water.

Our department, unlike some other departments, would pump cellars for the residents. With a limited number of pumps, we could only leave a pump in place for just so long and then it would be time to move to another house. Some people who have known water problems would have their own pumps in a sump, usually in the basement.

I remember going to a house one day for a water problem. The owner had only lived in the house for a short while. The house had a sump pump located in a closet in the basement playroom with piping to the outside. Trouble was, the pump wasn't working and the water was rising in the playroom. The owner had tried everything, or so he thought. He had even taken the discharge hose off to check for a clog.

I went in and decided to look at his pump before I left one that belonged to the fire department. His pump seemed as if it should be working, but it wouldn't come on. It was then that I spotted the switch on the wall. I flipped the switch and, that's right, the pump came on—and sprayed water everywhere! It seems that the man had forgotten to reconnect the discharge hose.

Well, I shut it off, helped the man reconnect everything, and then flipped the switch again. Bingo! Everything worked. It has always amazed me how little some people know about their own homes.

We also had some people with known water problems that decided to leave it to the fire department to take care of their problem for them. Every time the water came up, you'd see some of the same addresses on the list of those asking to be pumped. We would usually just set up the pump and leave it there, coming back to check it after a while. We had some people who didn't want to give back the pump, so they wouldn't answer the door when we came back. We would have to keep returning until they gave it back. Sometimes people would refuse to give back the pump. Then the police would have to come with us to get the pump back.

There were times when we would have just no place to put the water. Some homes along the river would have water pouring in the basement windows from their flooded yard. Pumping the water back out into their yard was not going to do any good. It would come right back in. In times like this we would have to tell the residents that we couldn't leave a pump. It was kind of like triage. We'd pump those that we could, but if water just came back in as fast as we pumped it out, we'd take the pump out.

I do remember one home we went to one night. The home was built on a flat piece of ground. I remember that area before the home was built. Horses would run in the field and drink from two spring-fed ponds. Then the land was sold, the ponds filled in, and houses built. But, the water table was high there. When we arrived, there was water pouring in through the basement windows. The owner had things in storage down there, and those things, as well as some very nice furniture, were floating around. We felt bad for him, so we put in one pump, then two, then three. We stayed there with three pumps working, but the water kept getting deeper. The captain finally told him that we'd have to take the pumps out because they were doing no good at that location, but they could do some good elsewhere.

The man panicked. He begged us to stay. Then he offered to buy the pumps from us. They weren't ours to sell and we told him so. Then he stood in our way and tried not to let us leave. He stopped that when he was threatened with the police. I remember the look on his face as we left. What can you do?

Sometimes, with limited resources, we just have to go where we will be able to do some good. Sometimes there's just nothing you can do.

Gas Explosion

One day late morning, working at station 2, we got a call for an explosion in a house on our side of town. My partner was driving. I slid into the passenger seat and we responded. We pulled out and turned left and left again. Then we could see it: a thick column of black smoke rising. It was about a mile away. We knew we had something.

We pulled up into the driveway of the house and found heavy fire rolling out of both sides of the two-car garage under the house. A box was struck on our report of smoke showing, and another engine was about four minutes away. I took an attack line to the garage doors and my partner prepared to give me the 500 gallons of water in the engine's tank. With this water, I started to attack the fire. I think we were using 1½" line then.

Things went well. I was able to knock down the fire in the garage and push it all back into a basement workshop area. I almost had it all put out when I ran out of water. The next engine was just pulling up to the hydrant. I lay down flat on the floor at the door leading from the garage into the basement, waiting for more water.

Then I heard a <BOOM> and a ball of fire came rolling out at me. Well, after I messed my pants, I left my line and started doing the backstroke across the floor toward the outside. I made it out as the fire rolled over my head. It was then that we were told it was a natural gas fire, started when a backhoe pulled the line out of the meter in the basement. It didn't take long for the house to go <BOOM>.

The gas company was pretty quick on scene, and we got more water on the fire and put it out. The house did not come apart, as often happens, but it did move on its foundation. There was too much damage to the structural members, so it had to come down.

Moral of the story? You can't extinguish a gas fire until the gas is turned off! Hell, I didn't know it was a gas fire. Maybe I should have asked. I did, however, discover that I could backstroke across a concrete floor quite well.

Get the Bolt Cutters

Part of our job is to do the inspections of local businesses, places of assembly, restaurants and town buildings, including the schools. The school system is very well thought of and has won awards and commendations. They tend to be very pleased with themselves. The school superintendent at the time of this story was, in my opinion, a very arrogant man who always thought he was right. What he wanted for his school system was what he wanted and the heck with everyone else. From what I heard, he never hesitated to get right in someone's face and tell them what was going to happen. People tended to be afraid to face him.

Sometimes there have been violations of fire code in the schools, but mostly the violations have been minor. There was one elementary school where we continuously found violations, such as storage of items in the hallways and partially blocked doors. The teachers also used to block their classroom doors open with wooden wedges. This was fine as long as the wedges were removed and the doors closed during fire alarms or when no one was in the room. They would also often wedge the fire doors in the hallways in the same manner. This is **never** permitted. Each time our inspectors saw this, they confiscated the wedges. After a great number of wedges had been collected, the school administration had the custodians place metal doorstops on some of the fire doors to hold them open, and chains on others so they could be fastened to the walls.

My duty shift and I went to this particular school one day for our quarterly inspection and found the doors blocked open with the stops and chains. The school was informed that this was a violation of fire code and a report was written by me. They were given two days to remove the chains and stops. Two days later, I went to the school to check for compliance with our order. Lo and behold, the doors were still held open. I left and returned to my office to write another violation report.

At the firehouse, I saw the chief of department and told him of the violation. He told me to come with him. He got into his car and told me to follow. We drove to the school. Before we entered the building, I was told to get the bolt cutters and a large screwdriver out of my toolbox. We went in and the chief told me to remove the stops and chains. While he stood in the office and talked to the office staff about the fire codes, I went to all the fire doors and either removed the stop or cut the chains off the wall. The custodian saw me and went toward the office, I guess to tell on me. When he saw the chief in there, the custodian must have changed his mind, because he disappeared. When I was done, the chief wrapped up his talk. We confiscated the stops and chains and took them with us when we left. There was no way *my chief* was afraid of the school superintendent!

Get the Scoop

Any one of us may wind up having to respond to a high profile call. Basically, this is a call where you want everything to go perfectly, or as close as you can get. Certainly we want all calls to go well, but with some, you're under the spotlight. For instance, these calls happen in places where the media is in abundance; they might be special kinds of calls, such as hazardous materials incidents, explosions or large fires; or they might involve well-known persons.

In the area where I worked, there are many celebrities from the sports world, news media, and politics, just to name a few. One afternoon some years back, I was on duty at station 1 when we got a request for the ambulance to a home for a possible hip fracture. My partner and I with the ambulance were first due and help was coming with the engine from station 2. The captain had been at station 2 with car 2 when we received the call and so he was responding from there.

I didn't recognize the address when we got the call, but when we arrived, I knew where we were. This was the home of an attorney who had been well known and in the political and media spotlight a few years before. Though not a politician himself, he was well known for having been appointed by a sitting president to investigate a national incident. At this time, the attorney was a professor at an internationally known law school.

We arrived and went inside and saw the attorney's wife sitting on the kitchen floor, conscious and alert and in some pain. She was the only one home and had been doing something in the kitchen. When she stepped back, she tripped over the dog and landed on the floor in a seated position. Her leg had the characteristic outward roll that indicated a possible hip fracture. That, coupled with the pain, made a fracture almost a sure thing.

Now, moving patients efficiently is a learned skill and also requires a bit of common sense. Many people would have gone for a long backboard, had her lay down on it, and secured her to the board. That's fine sometimes, but not now. The lady was seated and perfectly comfortable in that position. To try and lift her onto a board and lay her down on it would have aggravated her injury.

My partner didn't have nearly as much time on the job as me, but had enough experience so they should have been able to make a decision, but in this case, did not. I was the driver, so technically my partner should have been the one making the calls about patient care, but they didn't seem to know what to do.

With no decision coming, I asked them to go out and get the scoop stretcher. This is a piece of equipment that is about six feet long, is made of metal or plastic, and breaks in half the long way. The idea is to break this in half and insert it under the patient from both sides. When this has been done, it locks together and we can lift the patient to a stretcher with little movement.

After I made that call for the scoop, my partner didn't move but kept talking, both to me and to the patient. I requested that scoop a second time, and still got no response. Finally, I firmly told my partner to go out and get the scoop stretcher. This time they got up and went out to get the equipment. The station 2 engine and the captain were just arriving and asked my partner what was needed. My partner answered—somewhat sarcastically I'm told—that, "He wants the scoop stretcher. I have *no* idea why." The equipment was brought in, we secured her injured leg to the other leg for stability, used the equipment that I had requested to gently and easily lift the patient onto the ambulance cot, and transported her without any problem.

Some days later, the chief of department showed me a letter of thanks from this attorney for the efficient and professional way we had treated his wife. It was written on the stationary with the letterhead of the law school at which he taught.

This was a call that needed to go right the first time, and it did. There is no substitute for experience in our business, but you can't learn if you don't ever ask, "*Why?*" My partner never did.

Good Stop

I was working one night with the lieutenant at station 2. The alert tone from dispatch woke us around four in the morning. They dispatched us to a house fire on the other end of town. The fire was on a dead end street, off of a narrow, winding road. This is very quiet part of town, especially at night, so a fire could be burning for a considerable time before it is noticed.

The engine from station 1 signed off on the radio with heavy fire showing, and the captain, also on scene, called for the box to be struck for more help. We were the second engine in, so it was our job to find a hydrant and lay a supply line to the other engine. We went down the winding road, and just at the turn into the dead end street, there was a hydrant on the right. We stopped and the lieutenant got out, pulled off some 4-inch hose from the back, and hooked up the hose to the hydrant, while I drove in toward the fire, laying 4-inch hose as I went and helped with the connection to the engine.

The burning house was the last one on the street, right in the dead end. There was no one home and the fire had been going for a long time. It was a two-and-a-half-story house with a large, single story addition, mostly done, but still under construction. The addition was completely involved in fire. At this point, the addition was already lost and the fire was threatening the main house.

There were firefighters working, spraying water on the fire in the front of the house. I walked around to the back. The captain was there checking things out. As I came around the corner, I could see the fire working its way toward the main house. Then I looked up and saw a window and a chance to stop the fire. I heard another engine sign off at the fire as I pointed at the window and said to the captain, "Capt., if that window is closed, I think we can stop it right there."

He looked up, then said to me, "OK, take engine 4's crew and go up and stop it there." I went around front to engine 4 and told the crew that the captain said they were to come with me. Everyone got their breathing apparatus on and got their tools. We took an attack hose with us and in we went through the back door. The four of us found a stairway right inside the door. We went up and toward the fire.

When we reached the window, we found it closed, meaning that even though the fire had reached as far as the wall of the main house, that closed window had stopped it from passing through to the inside of the main house. We opened the wall between the house and the addition and found fire inside the wall, which we put out with our hose. We worked our way along the wall and put out any more fire we found in that wall.

We successfully prevented the fire from entering the main house. The addition was gone but we made a hell of a good stop and saved the main house. There's always an element of luck involved in making a stop like that, along with a lot of hard work. A good knowledge of fire behavior doesn't hurt either.

The Great Outdoors

I was on duty at headquarters one rather cold, winter afternoon some years ago, when we heard, over the radio, a neighboring fire department being dispatched for a house fire. The location was close enough to the town line that we had an assignment to respond with an engine company directly to the fire. The captain, the driver, and I got into our engine and responded.

We arrived to find a two-story house with heavy fire showing at most of the windows. We received our orders from the incident commander. After spending a bit of time knocking down fire on a rear porch and playing water into the upper story windows, we were finally ordered to take our hose line into the house and up to the second floor. We donned our breathing equipment, moved our hose to the front door, went on air and entered. The staircase was right in front of us as we went in. I had the nozzle and my partner was right on my tail, pulling hose up as we advanced.

Going up those stairs was tough. It was very hot and we could see flames above us. I opened the nozzle and played the water stream off the ceiling and toward the top of the stairs. As soon as the water hit the hot surfaces it turned to steam, and we no longer had any visibility. I stopped another couple of times on the way up to spray water and cool our atmosphere.

Finally, we reached the second floor. I saw fire off to my right and opened the nozzle. Suddenly, there was a gust of wind and the air cleared for a second. As I looked to my left, I realized that I was looking out onto the backyard, and I don't mean through a window. The fire had pretty much burned its way through the back wall, consuming much of what was once there. That kind of startled us. We realized that we probably shouldn't be there.

We worked our way back down the stairs, taking our hose with us. When we came outside, we met the incident commander as he was just coming to order us out. It was strange, sitting on the top of the stairs in a burning house, having the wind blow through and looking through where the wall had been, into the great outdoors. That's how quickly conditions can change in a fire situation. From the time we were ordered in until we reached the upper floor was really only a couple of minutes. In that short time, the fire had consumed the whole rear wall of the house. The house was a loss. A short time later, we were released by command to return to our own town.

Usually, for a few days after a fire, we would discuss and critique our performance. This time, however, we didn't have that luxury. A couple of days after this fire, there was a devastating fire in a cold storage warehouse in a city not too far from us. Six firefighters died in that fire. Two became lost while searching for homeless people reported to be in the structure, and the other four died while trying to search for and save their brothers. No homeless people were ever found in the building. That fire overshadowed ours and ours was quickly forgotten, and rightfully so. But I always remembered that trip up the stairs and my unexpected view of the backyard when I got there.

Ground Fog

Working at headquarters one day, I believe it was springtime, we received a call reporting a heavy cloud, or thick mist, in a marshy area in the north end of town. Callers reported that they thought it was some chemical that someone had disposed of in the marsh. My partner and I left from headquarters in our engine. The captain responded in car 2 while the engine from the south station was dispatched also.

We arrived in the area, a couple of miles away, to find a thick cloud of something hanging over the marsh. The chief had been in quarters and decided to respond in his car also. He was kind of a bull and kind of took things by the seat of the pants. He had a rather heavy foot while driving, so he got there before the rest of us and reported that it was "ground fog."

Well, there were many years of experience working that day, and none of us had ever seen any ground fog there at any time before. My partner was driving and pulled the engine up a dirt road to where we knew we could turn around. As we started back toward the marsh, we began to see something on the road. It was a trail of white powder in spots on the road leading back to the marsh. We started to get concerned when we heard the chief again reporting that it was "ground fog."

As we got nearer, we looked into the marsh. The chief had driven his car out into the marsh and was out and standing in the middle of whatever the fog was made up of. As he stood there and looked around, my partner and I looked at each other in disbelief. I sure hoped the chief was right about what it was; otherwise, he could be in trouble. After a while, the cloud started to disperse. We reported our finding of the white powder on the road to the captain. Where it went from there, I don't know. I'm sure he reported it to the chief, who didn't seem too worried about it. He called it "ground fog" and sent everyone back to quarters.

As it turned out, someone, I can't remember who, had spread agricultural lime in the marsh. I guess this was a good thing to do, though I don't remember the reason and there didn't end up being any problem. But as no one reported that they were applying the lime beforehand, none of us knew what we were dealing with. I'm not sure what the chief was thinking, but driving into the middle of the cloud and getting out of the car? That had disaster written all over it. Maybe he should just have let us handle it.

As an interesting side note, later that afternoon, the chief got a call from the dispatcher downstairs, who mentioned that call from that morning when the chief had said the cloud was "ground fog." The dispatcher then told the chief that there was a lady in the lobby with her son and the boy had that "ground fog" all over him! They cleaned him off and all was well. Never saw that fog again, thanks to the Great Spirit for small favors!

Gumby Suit

The firehouse can be a brutal place to work, especially during downtime. We are a group that feeds on each other. Anyone who knows us knows that the firehouse is not for the lighthearted or the thin-skinned. If something bothers you, leave it at the door when you come to work, along with your ego. Everyone is equal and everything is fair game. Laugh along and it goes away. Get mad and guess what...there's blood in the water and the sharks are circling. (Another common saying in the firehouse.)

One day we were training at the lake with the boats and water rescue equipment. We got through most of the material and only had the rescue suits to go. These were less-than-affectionately known as "Gumby suits." Yes, you looked like Gumby while wearing one. They were cumbersome in the water, but they *did* keep you afloat and grudgingly allowed you to work. It also was hard to enter the water while wearing one. To do it right, you really had to back into the water.

Well, this day the group had a man who was a bit on the heavy side. He was very conscious of his weight and all knew it. When it was his turn, he reddened and refused to put the suit on. Well, everything else being equal, he had the same job as the rest of us and so had to be proficient with the suit. So he was ordered to don the suit. This he did—grudgingly—as fast as he could, and started off at a brisk walk into the water. Walking forward and too fast, he soon tripped and fell down, creating a large splash and waves. Some smart-ass in the group yelled out, "THAR SHE BLOWS!!"

The man got up, left the water, pulled off the suit, and headed for the engine. I never saw him put that suit on again! Some folks just can't take it.

HAV Valve

Years ago, our department bought 4-inch hose. This is large diameter hose to better supply large amounts of water to the engines from the hydrant. It carries a lot of water and so has its own fittings and equipment. A captain in my own department was thoroughly confused by fire ground hydraulics and mystified by this hose. I had been using this hose for years working at the firefighting academy, but was not asked to teach the firefighters in my own town in its use. Another man from the department was asked.

When the class was over and the instructor had left, the captain called me over and asked what the big thing that goes on the hydrant was called. I said it was a "hydrant assist valve." He nodded and walked away.

A while later, the captain called us all together, gave me a dirty look, and said that he had just got off the phone with the one who had instructed us. The instructor told him that the piece was called a "HAV valve."

Then I said, "That's right, Capt. "HAV" H A V — hydrant assist valve." I got another dirty look and the training was over! Oh those benevolent officers of yesteryear! Think there are still any of them around?

Hawk Eye

Years ago, when I was first appointed to the fire department, some of the police officers in town were holdovers from a distant era and were not really up to modern standards, to say the least.

We all know that the skunk is a nocturnal animal, and if seen out during the day they are often sick. One day, the police department got a call from a citizen about a sick skunk. They had somehow trapped this animal in a metal trashcan with a lid. An officer responded. The can was on its side with the lid on. The officer decided that the animal should be destroyed. He drew his revolver, kicked the lid off the can, aimed and fired six (6) shots into the can at point-blank range.

Seconds later the skunk waddled out of the can and off into the woods, completely unharmed. I don't remember how officer Eagle Eye reacted or what he did. Maybe he should have gone to the range to practice!

Hiding the Dog

This is a story that I've told several times to recruits, but seems to be remembered fondly by many more people than I remember having told it to. One winter night after dark, but not too late, I was at home when the radio sent out the tone recalling all off duty firefighters back to duty. I responded on the recall from home to the firehouse and went to the fire on the next engine out the door.

A call had been received for a fire in one of the hundreds of condo units built in the large area on the south end of town. This condo was owned by a single young lady. She lived there with her dog. This evening she had gone out, leaving the dog at home. She had an electric space heater in the home, and the dog had a blanket on top of it to keep a little warmer. The best that anyone can figure is that the dog somehow disturbed the control on the heater, turning the temperature up very high. It eventually ignited the blanket. The fire spread a bit, but an early call reporting the fire got the fire department responding quickly into the incident. A quick, effective attack stopped the fire, but left much heat and smoke damage throughout the home. Tragically, the dog did not survive.

As we were overhauling the fire scene, the owner arrived home. She was very visibly upset by what had happened, crying as she looked around. The captain came to me and said that she didn't need to see her deceased dog lying in the living room. He ordered me to take it out to the backyard. I obliged and carried it outside and put it down. I looked back and saw that it really stood out as a dark shape on the white snow at night. So I came up with a master plan. I reached inside the house and off the floor I took a fairly small rug, went out and covered the dog's body. Shortly after, my engine was sent back to quarters.

Well, the next week when I came to work, I was called into the chief's office. He asked me to explain what I had done with the dog, which I did. Then the chief asked where I had gotten the rug. I told him that I had gotten it from the floor, just inside the back door. It was then that he told me that the rug was a very valuable Persian rug, and the lady of the house was pretty upset at finding it outside, covering the body of her dead dog. There were no repercussions, but I must have been removed from both of their Christmas card lists. I never got a birthday card from her or the department, either! Oh well.

Hometown

Staying and working in the same town where you grew up is kind of a double-edged sword. On one hand, you know the town and its people. You know the layout and where clusters of different kinds of people live. It's a short trip to work: a short drive, a bicycle ride or even a walk on a nice day. You're comfortable working in your hometown.

On the other hand, sometimes fires damage or destroy the home of someone you're familiar with. Sometimes you know the person who is sick, injured, or killed. They might be the parents of friends and classmates, or maybe the friends themselves.

I have relatives buried in a large cemetery in town. I sometimes go to visit. I remember that place when it was much smaller. I used to go there often while playing in the woods around the lake as a kid. Now the place has grown, and as I walk through, I see names that I know—old friends and classmates or their parents. I remember being with some of these people at the time they died. Sometimes it was a real mess, sometimes very neat and clean. Often there was nothing we could do because we got there too late.

Sometimes I just sit and look around and remember. I remember taking a next-door neighbor, the lady of the house, to the hospital for the last time. I had known her all my life. She had been sick a long time. We got the call in the midmorning in a raging snowstorm. We backed the ambulance up my own driveway, because even running through the drifting snow, it was the easiest and quickest way to get her out. She died at the local hospital.

The father of a good friend was depressed and attempted suicide one morning. He was found in time, and as they took him to the hospital, he was heard to utter, "Next time I won't miss." I had spent much of my teenage years and early 20s at that house with my friend, and his parents were always great to be around. Some months later, I was coming on duty at 0800 one morning, when the off-going shift told me about a call they had. The man had tried again. He was right, that time he didn't miss.

I have seen people I know die in fires, get hit and killed by cars, and I have helped as they were injured or sick. Some lived, some did not. There was a friend I had in school, whose house I had been at and had met his parents many times. As we grew a bit older, my friend and I didn't see each other much, but his parents still lived in town, in the same house. Then his father passed on. I believe he had been sick. I think he died in the hospital. His mother lived in the old house. After a time, she developed a severe heart problem and had several major heart attacks. She would call for help when she had chest pain. If I was on duty when she called, I would come in and talk to her and sometimes jokingly scold her for walking around and doing chores while having pain. She grew comfortable with me. She eventually moved into elderly housing, but the heart attacks continued.

Finally, one night she called us with chest pain. I arrived in the ambulance and entered her apartment. She was lying on the bed in distress. I walked in and said, "Hello." She raised her head, looked at me, opened her mouth and fell back in full arrest. We did what we always did when this happened, and when we got her to the local hospital our work seemingly paid off—we had a pulse. But we had no illusions. She was too sick and there had been too much damage for her to recover, even with help immediately available. Her heart stopped and they got her back several times while we were still at the hospital, but finally it was all over. We returned to the firehouse.

Later, after we went to bed, the dispatcher came over the speaker and said that I had a phone call. I got up and answered. It was my old friend and classmate. He thanked me for trying so hard on his mother. He asked me questions about what happened and asked if there were any last words. There were not.

I never had much trouble doing the calls and dealing with what I found there, but talking to a victim's family and friends has never been my strong point. I can do it, but it's often hard to find the words. I guess that's one of the downsides of staying in one place. Still, if I had a do-over, I wouldn't change a thing.

Hornets

I was working an overtime day shift in the late spring many years ago when we got a call for the ambulance for a man who had taken a fall. We arrived to find the south side engine already there. There was a tree company bucket truck with the bucket partially in the air and a man lying on the ground, face down, and not moving.

What we didn't see at the time were the hornets. It seems that the tree men were trimming trees. The branches were full of new leaves. The man in the bucket cut a branch and it fell, revealing a large, white-faced hornet's nest on the branch. These are nasty creatures and they were all over him in an instant. The bucket didn't move fast enough, so he tried to jump out to get away. The bottom of the bucket was only about 8 ft. or so above the ground, making a controlled jump safe. The trouble was that he caught his foot on the edge of the bucket as he jumped, turning him to fall face first and head down. He hit, breaking his neck instantly. He was alive and conscious, but felt nothing as he was repeatedly stung.

One of our firefighters was allergic to bee stings. Although he had his epi-kit, there were far too many hornets for the epi to be useful. So, with one man having to keep his distance, we began to use CO_2 fire extinguishers on the nest to allow us to work. We quickly lifted him about 2 inches off the ground and slid a backboard under him while stabilizing his neck. It is not common practice, but since his airway was fine, and in the interest of time, we secured him to the board face down. Transport time was only about 4 to 5 minutes.

At the hospital, under the direction of the emergency room physician, we put another board on top of him, that is, on his back, sandwiching him between two boards. We secured it in place and turned him over. He had no feeling from his neck down and was covered with stings.

This had been an unusual call. We did our reports and left. I lost track of what happened to him, but I never forgot him. Here was a healthy, strong, thirty-year-old man doing hard work, and suddenly he's in the hospital, paralyzed.

The story doesn't end there. Some years after, I was working a side job with a local ambulance company. Late one day we were given a call to go to a Boston hospital to return a patient home to a western suburb. We got to the hospital and found that our patient was a youngish man in a wheelchair. He was paralyzed in the lower body but had limited use of his arms and hands. He rode on the stretcher and we stowed his chair.

During the trip, I talked to him, and through conversation I found that this was the same man from that call years before. Things had not worked out too well for him, but he seemed to have a good, upbeat attitude. I felt terrible that this is how things had turned out. It's not often that we get this kind of a look at what has become of our patients.

Some months after that, I was home and received in the mail a deposition subpoena. I was to appear at a lawyer's office to recount the events that had occurred on our original call some years earlier, when that man had gotten stung and fell. It seems that this man's outlook had not been as upbeat as I had thought.

One day, while home alone, he had put a pistol in his mouth and pulled the trigger, killing himself. His mother was suing everyone she could think of for wrongful death. I never found out how things turned out, but the whole situation was out of the ordinary and very sad.

I Know the Way Out

If you're really into the job, working at the MFFA is a firefighter's dream. You get to learn, play with fire, teach, and get paid for it, too. I was lucky. I almost always got to work in the burn building during live burn training. I guess I got pretty good at it.

I remember walking up the hill toward the burn building one morning to build and light the fires for that day. My bunker gear was all scorched and burned and all the Velcro had burned away, so parts of the coat would no longer fasten. My red helmet was burned black and the face shield was melted into some weird shape.

At the top of the hill stood the incident commander. He was the man in charge of burn operations for that day. He was talking to one of the recruits, and as I approached, he looked up at me and said, "Oh no, not *you*!" It was said with a smile on his face. He knew it was going to be a good day. However, I always chuckle when I remember the look of apprehension on the face of the recruit. He didn't know what to expect. The instructor knew!

I always liked to build and light fires in the basement best. I had a fire that I designed. It was built against a wall near the stairwell leading upstairs, but around the corner so it couldn't be put out from the stairs. The students would have to get down the stairs with the hose and turn the corner as they came out of the stairwell. I built a kind of V shape with pallets and also placed a pallet on top. This way, I could put straw into the V and on top of it. The whole thing was built on metal racks to get it off the floor. I also stuffed straw on the lower shelf of the rack. The whole thing probably took five bales of straw, which I broke apart so it would burn better. For good measure, I broke apart a bale at the top of the stairs and kicked it down, covering the stairs with straw also. I would open the door at the top of the stairs and one at the basement level, and with the breeze that always seemed to be blowing, we could send everything; heat, smoke, and flames; up into the stairwell, just to make things as difficult as possible. What the hell, they gotta learn! This was one hot fire every time I built it.

One day, I had just lit this fire and the students were coming with their hose. They moved pretty fast, but it always seemed to take them forever to get there. I had lit the stairwell, then the big fire, and was standing at the bottom of the stairway with the big fire behind me. I was keeping the stairs burning hot and the big fire was getting bigger when I started to feel increasing heat through my gear. That gear will only protect just so far.

Well, I knew it was time to leave. The whole room was now full of smoke and flame and I couldn't see. That was alright because I knew the way out. I turned around and ran, low to the next corner, then turned to my right. I knew the door was in a straight line from where I was. I was really feeling the heat now, and had to get out fast. I crouched down and ran for the door. <BONK!> I ran head first into the wall! I said I knew the way out, and I did! It was about a foot to the right of where I was. I'm just thankful for helmets!

I Rode the Step

When I first started in the fire service, we wore ¾ boots, rubber gloves, canvas coats with removable wool liners, and helmets without impact caps. We had limited breathing equipment, and we did it all while riding standing on the back step. The cab was occupied by the driver, the officer, and maybe one butt-kisser (if there was enough room). The rest of us backstepped it. We complained about it then: the rain blowing in your face as we raced along, the snow as it fell down your neck, the freezing rain as it numbed your face and formed icicles on your eyebrows and mustache. We would duck down as far as possible to cut down the wind in your face, all the while holding on with your arm hooked around the upper bar and your hands balled up inside your gloves or mittens to keep them warm.

We'd ride this way across town from the outstation to cover the headquarters station if they were at a fire. Back then, there was no communication between the guys on the step and the people up front in the cab. There were also no automatic transmissions in the apparatus. You'd be riding the step and you'd hear the downshift and feel the engine pick up speed. Then you knew we had been redirected to go to the fire. The excitement and expectation would build and you wouldn't be cold any more.

In the nicer, warmer weather, the step was a place you could enjoy the ride and see things as you approached. On the way back, the step was a quiet place and time where we could reflect on where we had just been and what we had done.

We complained about it—then. Now it's a place of honor to have ridden. To have been a part of fire history that is pretty much gone. The old-timers talk with pride of the days when they "rode the step." The youngsters who are coming on the job now will never experience that thrill. My department only does it now at Christmas time when we do Santa's Ride. A few days before Christmas, Santa rides on the fire engine to visit the children in town. Several firefighters go along to assist him, and they ride the step.

My last time was on such a ride. It was a rainy, misty night. The other "elves" elected to ride in a pickup truck following so they could keep dry. I chose to ride on the step. It was a magnificent night. I was alone there with all my thoughts and memories. It was my final time. I am honored to have been a part of that time, to be able to say, "I rode the step." These new guys will never know...

I Work In Car

Back in the olden days, extricating an injured person from a wrecked automobile was no easy task. It was done with hand tools: axes, pry bars, hacksaws and anything else that you could think of to get the job done. After a while, someone invented the Port-A-Power system. This was a collection of chains, hooks, and prying equipment operated hydraulically with a hand pump. It was still not power equipment, but it was a damn site better that what was being used before.

Sometime in the early 70s, as I remember, the Hurst Company came out with the "Jaws of Life." It was a component system made up of a power unit, hydraulic lines and all kinds of attachments. The attachments could be hooked up and used to bend, cut, push, etc. and do the many things that needed to be done at a motor vehicle accident. This tool was heaven-sent. Several different companies now make similar hydraulic tools. Just about every fire department has one, and some have more than one.

Our department got one in the mid 70s when the local Kiwanis Club donated the money to us. The unit was used many, many times over the years. The tool has been redesigned and modified many times to make it lighter and easier to use and more versatile. Since we now had a tool that could perform and do what needed to be done quickly, new standard operating procedures have been developed to better organize rescue at an MVA and get the patient to the hospital much more quickly.

I was working on the engine at station 2 on the south side one afternoon when we got a call for an MVA about a mile from the firehouse. It was on a side street, but a busy one. Our response was to send the ambulance and the captain in car 2, as well as the engine company from the south side for extra manpower.

The ambulance arrived to find a full size car, I think it was a Crown Victoria, head-on into a tree. There was substantial damage to the car and they could not open the doors. There was only one person in the car. It was a rather small, Asian man who spoke broken, heavily-accented English, so there was a real communication barrier. We noticed that the entire car, except where the driver sat, was filled with boxes of papers, kind of a collection of files stored in boxes.

The south side engine arrived and we looked things over. The vehicle was into the trees on the roadside making entry through a door difficult, if it were even possible to pry one open.

We elected to cut the roof completely off. This would give us full access to the patient and make extrication possible. The patient was injured and the mechanism of injury indicated he could be severely injured, so speed was important. There were no paramedics available to respond. We set up the Jaws, cut through the posts holding the roof, and lifted the roof from the vehicle. We checked the patient for vital signs and bleeding and made sure he had good air exchange. The patient was trying to speak to us but it was difficult to understand.

The boxes in the car were open topped and the wind began to blow some of the papers around. With only five firefighters plus the officer, there was no one to pick the papers up right away. The patient was placed on and secured to a long backboard and his neck stabilized with a collar. The extrication went smoothly. It was decided to send the patient into Boson due to the injury potential.

As the patient was being placed in the ambulance, he suddenly blurted out, "I work in car." I looked back and saw the papers scattered around and his car in ruins. As I helped to load the patient into the ambulance, I didn't have the heart to tell him that we just cut the roof off of his office.

Ice Rescue

I became the department training officer about the time I made lieutenant and kept the position until I retired. There is always the in-service training that we have to do to keep up with tools and procedures. This is important because you never know what's going to happen next and you have to be ready. Of course, there are always the things that are too big or too specialized for us to handle, like confined space rescue or hazardous materials incidents. We then can usually call a team of specialists.

The training officer should also try to bring in other things of use and interest. I was lucky in that I worked at the state firefighting academy. This gave me access to instructors and classes that might otherwise be hard to get. We have a lot of water in town in the form of a large lake, a river, and very many smaller ponds scattered through the town. The fire department is responsible for water rescue. We have boats, floatation rescue suits, ropes, and floats, etc. We drilled with this equipment pretty often.

In New England, it gets cold in the winter and the water freezes. Among the more common ice-related problems is when a person is walking their dog and the dog runs onto the ice. If the dog falls through, the owner will often run out on the ice to rescue the dog. This would be fine except that if the ice wasn't strong enough to hold the dog, it will not be strong enough to hold the owner.

We were theoretically responsible for ice rescue in our town. Trouble was, we had no real plan in place. We'd gotten lucky that we hadn't had a major ice rescue incident. Trouble is, we were on borrowed time. We were overdue for something to happen on the ice. Could we handle it? Maybe, but without procedures in place, it could be dangerous, even tragic.

One fall, while attending a class put on by the firefighting academy, I started talking with one of the instructors. She was a firefighter from the western part of the state. While talking, I mentioned that I wanted to get a good ice rescue class for our department. As things turned out, she and her husband also taught for an organization that teaches ice and water rescue classes. Before she left, I had made arrangements to contact her that winter and put together a course in ice rescue designed for our department. I spoke with the chief and he gave the go ahead.

Before winter, however, we got a new chief. I explained things to him and he agreed that this would benefit us. He managed to get a state grant and asked me what we needed for equipment. We gave him a list and soon the things started to come in. I got in touch with another man on our department who was interested in training and was good at organizing and planning. We put together a class for our people.

Next, we had to contact our instructor. I gave her a call. The plan called for her to come to us and stay overnight in our spare room. She would have to do this twice to catch all four shifts for the classroom work. Then we planned a day for the practical work at the town beach. This involved cutting holes in the ice and putting "victims" in survival suits, into the water. Then we had rescue teams in rescue suits approach with ropes, get in the water with the "victims," and rescue our "victims."

The day was very successful. We had all worked together and developed an ice rescue plan for our department based on our manpower and equipment and it worked great. Most members of the department took the training and we became certified ice rescue technicians. Now the department is prepared with trained personnel, equipment, and established procedures. What a lucky twist of fate that I happened to meet that instructor when I did.

It Ain't For Everybody

Our department, I suppose like all other small fire departments, has a minimum number of people on duty at a time: enough to get started dealing with an emergency. Then we depend heavily on callback, that is, people coming back from off duty to help. The department issues us small radio receivers for our homes that operate when the dispatcher sends out a tone alert over the radio. Then the receivers self-activate and we are notified of the emergency so we can come back to work. It's mostly for fires, but not only that.

For the blizzard of 1978, the department sent out the tone calling everyone back for station coverage before the roads became impassable. Some emergency calls require more help, and if the roads are covered with deep snow, additional help wouldn't be able to get back to the firehouse. In the case of the blizzard, they wanted us to leave our own cars at home. They came and picked us up in a department vehicle.

Well, very early one very cold Christmas morning, my telephone rang. It was the fire department calling people back for a fire. Something had gone wrong and many of the home receivers did not open up to alert us, mine being one of them. I don't remember what the temperature was, but I know it was well below zero. My callback assignment was station 1. I walked in and was told to get geared up. The chief was sending a vehicle back to take a bunch of us to the fire to relieve the people that had been there a while. They needed a break and to get warm.

As I was putting on my bunker gear; pants, coat, hood, heavy socks under the boots, and last, but not least, mittens; I saw, standing near me, a call man. He was wearing his coat, helmet, and a pair of the high boots that we used at that time in the warmer weather. He had no gloves. One might say he wasn't too well prepared. We had been issued some of the best mittens that money could buy. But, at that time, firefighting gloves hadn't been invented. You used whatever gloves you wanted. I only had a pair of unlined, leather gloves in my pockets, but as I was wearing mittens, I offered him the gloves. Having nothing else, he took them. Our transportation arrived, the cold men got off, we got on and off to the fire we went. Man, it was cold!

The fire was in a structure that housed a small barn with horses and living quarters above. I remember the fire had started because of a wiring problem in the barn. Barns usually burn very well. The people upstairs had woken to the sound of the horses in the barn. They called us and got out. Some of the horses were saved, but tragically, four horses died. We were there for quite a while and finally the fire was declared under control.

Often after a difficult fire, we leave what we call a "fire watch" on scene for a while to make sure there are no flare-ups. The watch for this fire was another firefighter, myself, and that call man who I had given the gloves to. We walked around the fire scene checking things out for about three hours after everyone had gone back to the firehouse. They brought us hot coffee, but mostly we walked around in the cold and ice. The other guy and I were pretty well dressed for this and we were still cold. That poor call man froze. If nothing else, he was learning a lesson about being prepared. They came and got him a bit earlier than us, but around noon we were picked up and released to go home. It took a long time to thaw out after that.

Now, that call man was pretty well thought of by most of the guys as well as the chief and the officers. He was a local guy who everyone knew. He was a builder and was known as a hard worker. So, a short while later when a full-time job opened up, it was offered to him. It's a good job with pretty good pay and enough time off to continue his building job. He must have remembered the Christmas morning he had spent with us in the cold. He probably remembered how he suffered in that cold. He said, "No thanks." Lesson learned and no repeats. Oh well, the job ain't for everybody.

It's All Greek to Me

Yet another story, torn from the pages of "What Were the Chances..." Years ago, while working in the private ambulance service one afternoon, I was sent to a Boston area nursing home to transport a patient to a Boston hospital. It was a routine transport and not an emergency. I was working with a young lady (I was younger then, too) who I knew well and was a good friend of mine. It was supposed to be her turn to drive. When we got to the nursing home, I got the chart and started the paperwork that always accompanied these trips. When I was done and before I had seen the patient, the nurse told me that there would be a problem: the patient didn't speak English. That wasn't really unusual, so I asked what language he spoke. I was told that he spoke only Greek.

As I remember, I looked up and smiled. I verified that Greek was his language and heaved a sigh of relief. By pure chance, my partner that day happened to be the only person in the whole company that spoke fluent Greek. I told her and she went into the room and began to talk to the patient. I think *he* was relieved, too, that someone could talk to him.

Well, I did the driving on that transport while my partner and the patient carried on a conversation. The trip was made without incident. What the hell were the chances that *we* would be the ones sent to that call?

Δεν μιλώ Ελληνικά.

Key in the Rock

We have in our jargon what we call "frequent flyers." These are people who frequently call for the ambulance. Of these, some legitimately need help, though there is not always an emergency. There are some who abuse the system. They call because they believe that arriving at the hospital by ambulance means that they will be seen sooner. That is not the case. The ER will see patients in the greatest need first. There are people who want us to come and do chores and provide personal care for them while they sit and watch. There are those who call whenever they have any little ache or pain. Some are just old and lonely and seek any company, including ambulance crews and hospital staff.

We try to be understanding and accommodating, but sometimes we have someone who is just a miserable person, full of curses, accusations, and unrealistic expectations. We had one that we dreaded getting a call from. We hardly ever took this person to the hospital. We rarely found any sickness or injury. This person was a miserable person to deal with, but they did have real problems, yet almost never of an emergency nature. Nothing was ever good enough. There was even a specific way that we were supposed to enter the home. There was an electric garage door that opened with a key inserted into a slot on the doorframe. Then we were to enter the garage and enter the house through the door that led into the kitchen from there. *No exceptions!* This person kept the key in a fake rock among the real rocks in a rock garden out in the backyard.

One winter we had had a large snowstorm, there were power outages all over, and we were busy. Sure enough, we got a call from that dreaded address. We got there and went around back. We were able to communicate by yelling at a window. The patient was on the floor, not injured, but in need of help getting back into a recliner. Well, due to the snow, we couldn't find the "rock," and even if we had, there was no power for the garage door.

We yelled through the window that we'd have to force our way in, to which the person responded, "No!" We were *not* to break anything! After some minutes of argument, the person said, "Wait a minute."

As we watched, the person got up, walked to the window, opened a small shutter, and unlocked the window. They then went back over by the chair and lay back on the floor. I would never have believed the audacity if I hadn't seen it myself!

Well, the captain looked and said, "There's nothing wrong with you!" and told us to return to quarters. I'm told that the next day, as soon as the town hall opened, the resident was there with tales of abuse at the hands of our captain, who had allegedly cursed and slapped the resident's face. Funny, I was there, but I never saw any such thing. Talk about abuse of the system!

Last Support Fire

Working at the fire academy was training for us while we taught others. Some time ago, I worked in support services. What that means is that although we worked with the recruits, support people did not directly teach. We set up and ran the equipment, and so we got very good with the tools of the trade. We built and lit the fires and kept them burning, yet didn't have to guide a crew in to fight the fire. So not having students to worry about, we could watch and see what the fires did and how they behaved. In this way, we developed a good understanding of fire behavior. We listened and learned from the instructors who told the students how to fight fire, and got paid for it. It was some of the best training anyone could get. We got pretty good at those burns, too, and with that came other lessons to be learned.

There was a time before the academy started worrying about expenses. We had no real restrictions in the amount of fuel we could use for our fires, and we sometimes made them big. All we burned was straw and wood pallets. If it doesn't sound like much, talk to some of our past recruit veterans of our fire training! It burned fast and hot, and we could rebuild the fires quickly during the day.

Before I changed jobs and became an instructor, I worked one final burn day alongside an old friend. We had worked together for years building these fires. He was going to stay in support services for a while, so we decided to make our last fire together a memorable one.

On the top floor of our burn building, there was just one big room with one staircase. There were two ladders leading up to roof hatches. There was a bunch of windows, but only one could be used for escape as it led to a balcony on a fire escape. What we usually did was light our fire, make sure it was going well, and at the last minute we'd dive out that window onto the balcony.

Well, my friend and I did it right. We built some huge structure by leaning and piling pallets. Then we broke up thirteen bales of straw and stuffed our structure. That fire was huge. We opened what windows we needed to give enough air to the fire. We lit the fire at the right time. It was a windy day and as the fire took off, the wind started blowing hard through a window we had opened. It blew the fire toward our escape window, filling it with fire. The fire was between us and the staircase. The fire was getting bigger and very hot as we looked for a way out.

There wasn't any easy way, so my friend said, "So this is how it ends. See you in hell." Then he got into a corner and lay prone with his face in his arms: a survival position. Well, with no place else to go, I joined him on the floor. Of course, this was pretty much a controlled burn and we were never really without a way out. It would have been work, but we could have gotten out if we had to. Besides, we knew there was a hose line coming up the stairs any second.

We kept our faces buried in our arms and could hear the designated inside safety instructor laughing at our predicament. Then the hose came up. Trouble was that they didn't expect this kind of heat and came up standing too high. The heat drove them back down the stairs. They regrouped, came up again, and this time they knocked the fire down. Then they opened all the windows, and the room cooled down.

It had been hot and things didn't work exactly as planned. But, at least we got a chance to practice survival techniques! We were nuts in those days!

Lawn Ornament Fire

Years ago, while on duty at station 2, we were dispatched to a home at the far northern border of the town for a "lawn ornament fire." Now, this was about a six mile run for us to the other side of town, and we couldn't imagine why we were being sent to a fire in a lawn jockey or garden gnome or something small like that, as we imagined a lawn ornament to be. About halfway there we could see the glow in the sky that told us that we were going to something somewhat larger than a lawn jockey. We arrived on scene to find a three-story structure in a backyard with flames rolling out every window. We went to work and a neighboring town showed up to lend a hand. After what seemed a very long time, we had the fire out.

We then found out that the person who owned the property was an artist who constructed this thing: tall and thin, three stories high, with windows and doors, made from wire, plaster, and lumber, and simulated lights made from wine bottles. It was his version of a spaceship. A *spaceship*!! Earlier in the day, he had found some kids playing there and had chased them away. They must have returned and set the fire.

I have to jump through hoops for a permit to build more space for my family to live, and he gets to build a spaceship in his yard! Well anyway, I remain one of the few firefighters in the area to have fought a spaceship fire during my career.

Locks Were Made for Honest People

People, being what they are and not always at their brightest at any given time, sometimes manage to lock themselves out of their homes and cars. It's part of our job to assist when called. Usually, there are common tools that can be used and a few specialty tools for those other times. After a few years of doing this, you get pretty good at breaking into things with little or no damage.

One very rainy Saturday morning years ago, I responded with the captain in the car to a house lockout. It seems that the chairperson of the board of selectmen had managed to lock herself out of the house. We arrived in the pouring rain and found her there, waiting for us and getting soaked. No one was very happy about being there in the rain. I walked around the house, looked things over, came back and got the toolbox. I found what I needed, then went to a window in the rear of the house. I won't say how I did it, (it was really easy!) but the lady of the house was dumbfounded when, seconds later, I walked out the front door of her house. She was ecstatic and asked how I had gotten in.

I answered, "Can't tell you—trade secret." The captain laughed and jokingly told her that I used to break into houses before I got on the fire department. It was raining too hard for her to argue, but she *did* have a few things to say about all those expensive locks and alarms she had had installed, and how I was able to get inside that quickly. I simply said, "Locks were made for honest people." She smiled and went inside.

Well, locks *were* made for honest people!

Long Lug Out

In our business, there's no substitute for experience. However, training in the basics plays a big part, too. We teach the recruits at the fire academy a self-rescue technique called "long lug out." It's for a firefighter who is lost in a fire situation and may be lucky enough to have or find a hose line. If they look at the hose couplings, it will show them the way out.

A line of hose sections is attached together with couplings. Each coupling has a male part and a female part. The female part threads onto the male part. It has short, rounded lugs on the outside. The male part has long lugs that span the length of the coupling and run parallel to the hose. Under normal circumstances, the hoses are used in the same orientation. The female side is closer to the nozzle end of the hose and the male end is always closer to the engine. The idea is that a firefighter can find a set of couplings, and using his gloved hands, can feel the lugs. The short ones are on the female half. They tell that the nozzle is in that direction. The long lugs on the male half point the way toward the pump. Following the long lugs along that line of hose will point the way out to the engine. It works well, once you get the hang of it.

When I was a lieutenant, we were able to get an abandoned house to drill in—no burns, but almost anything else you could think of. The captain and I took the group to the house and had some productive drill time for the afternoon. One of the last things we did was a 'long lug out' drill. The crew were all graduates of the fire academy. I was, too, plus I was also a recruit instructor. This particular captain was neither.

We, the officers, got some hose and ran it through the house in loops and twists, up and down stairs, around corners, and any other way we could think of to confuse the troops. We blacked out the face pieces on their SCBA, led them into the house, turned them around a few times to confuse them, and we turned them loose. They all performed well. They found the hose and followed the long lugs out.

Then the troops decided to do the same for us, their officers. They went in and moved the hose around. When they were ready, they took the captain and me in with blacked out face pieces, turned us around a couple of times, and left us. I found the hose rather quickly and followed it to a coupling. I felt the lugs and determined the way out. The captain did not follow. He decided to rely on dead reckoning. He called to me and asked me where I was. I told him that I had the hose and to follow my voice.

He said, "No," and said that I should follow his voice as he thought he knew the way out. I stayed with the hose. He called out to me a few more times instructing me to come with him, again insisting that he knew the way out.

I said that I was staying with the hose. After another few minutes, he called to me again. This time he said he was lost and wanted me to keep talking so he could find the hose. I did and soon he was right behind me and we felt our way along using the lugs to show us the way. We soon found our way out.

You can only imagine what could, and probably would, have happened in a real fire situation if this man got lost and performed the way he did in this drill. We probably would have had to send in a rescue team to save him, if he were lucky. It's likely we would have found his body after the fire. Practice like you play and always fall back on your basics. They'll save your ass nearly every time.

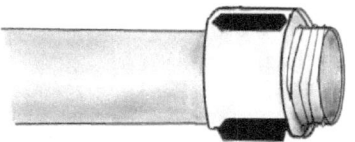 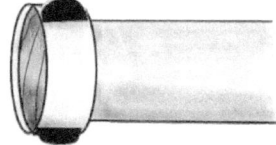

Malfunctioning Smokes

Working one night shift as the duty captain, I responded alone in car 2 to a call for smoke detectors sounding in a home. The residents were home and had said there was no fire. It was about 10 p.m. and I could hear the detectors screaming from outside the house.

I rang the bell and was greeted by a woman in an absolute rage who yelled at me for the fire detector system that I made her put in, as the detectors continued to sound. The system that I *made her* put in! This was a newer home and quite large, so there were a large number of detectors required and they all had to be hard wired. That means they are wired into the electrical system for the house, and they were all wired together. When one goes off, they all do. It made a racket.

I walked inside and saw a man and two children huddled together on the sofa, clearly afraid of this rampaging wild woman that I'm sure was normally a loving wife and mother. Not tonight though. I tried to explain that it probably was just a malfunctioning detector. All she needed to do was look at the detectors until she found the one that was lit up and that would be the malfunctioning one.

Well, she didn't want to hear it, so I went looking. There must have been a dozen detectors, a relatively small number for a new house in that town. I finally found it. It was the *last* detector to check. It was lit up bright. I took it down and the noise stopped. I explained that all she had to do was go out and get a replacement and just put it in. Then I smiled, she went, "Humph!" and I left. The nerve of *me* making her put in that evil system.

A Man I Used to Know

There are many different kinds of people that take a job with the fire department. In the olden days, it might have been for security, a steady paycheck. Some take it because they want to wear the suit, others because they really want to do the job.

Of all the different kinds of people I've met, there's one man that stands out. He was older, almost my father's age. He'd grown up in a rather large family in the city. He was a pure, working-class man, hard as nails. He didn't have those rugged good looks that you see and hear about. He was short, slouched, and looked rather generally beat up, yet I think he was one of the hardest, toughest men I've ever known. He was a nice, friendly man, always laughing, but he liked to get physical. Never content with a simple handshake, he'd gently crush your hand. Sometimes...no, often, he would grab a few chest hairs and pull, or get a pinch of skin just to make you yell. Purple nurples were a particular favorite of his. He twisted ears as well. All in good fun, of course. Getting a "rub down" from him was usually not very pleasant, but you'd laugh while trying to get away from him. We had no females on our department then, so he never had to worry about who or what he was grabbing. The guys would goad him into making a grab for one of them, then run away yelling as he laughed and chased them.

One day he walked into station 2. There were several other guys hanging around. When he walked in, they all pounced on him, about six of them. Down he went—with all those guys on top of him. Then he stood up—with all those guys hanging onto him. It was then that they all knew they had made a big mistake and someone was going to have to pay. They grabbed one guy and pushed him closer to the man and all the rest ran. The one that they chose to sacrifice was a very hairy man, every place but his head. They said you could hear the poor man screaming as he received one of the dreaded rubdowns and hair-pulls.

In the military, this man was a paratrooper, he jumped out of planes. However, sometime after that Lady Luck kind of walked out on him. His 5th day on the fire department he was injured—burned. Most of the guys who were off duty that night were at the bachelor party of another firefighter.

The man in our story was new. He didn't know anyone too well, so he didn't go to the party. That night there was a fire on my street. It was 1965 and I remember seeing the fire. Our friend was trapped by the fire in the attic and he suffered 2nd degree burns on his legs. He was out of work for six months.

Another time, while plowing his own driveway one winter, he sideswiped a tree. The door opened and he fell and almost ran over himself. He got away with some scrapes and bruises.

While building his own home, he fell from the ridgepole and landed on the concrete basement floor. This time he broke his back. He recovered from that and came back to work.

He was always doing hard work. He was a man who could pick up your refrigerator and carry it out, yet he also had the patience to hang wallpaper. I was very thankful for that one day when I tried to hang wallpaper and wasn't having much luck. He came to my house during his dinner hour to help me get started.

You probably didn't want him to do any painting for you though. He was kind of messy. Sometimes he was kind of clumsy. He'd trip and fall but always bounced right back up laughing. He often would turn up in the wrong place.

I remember an MVA when we had the Jaws working on a car door. We were working on the pin so the door would swing on its hinges when it opened. Well, where do you think I saw our friend standing? That's right, in line with the door. Before anyone could say anything, the door popped open—hard— and hit him. It knocked him off his feet and threw him back a short way. It probably would have broken something on an average man, but not him. He stood up, dusted himself off, and went right back to work. Nothing else said.

He could endure this, and yet when he tried to ride his bicycle to work one day, he wiped out in the sand. The guys saw him walking in, covered with blood and scratches and carrying the bike.

One summer evening, I was at station 1 when we got a call for an injury at the girls' softball game across town. Our friend was on the engine from station 2 and was first due and we were coming with the ambulance. Well, it turned out that a girl had injured a knee while sliding into second base. She was still seated on the ground near the base. Our friend decided to apply a full leg air splint. That would have been a good idea, but he got out a full *arm* splint instead. The difference didn't even occur to him. The absence of a foot on the splint went unnoticed as he applied it to the girl's leg and pulled it up to the knee. It was a little short, but I guess it was OK with him. No harm done, really.

These splints have an air valve and have to be blown up by mouth. Well, where do you think the valve was? He had it high on the leg, on the inside. When we came around the corner in the ambulance, we saw the girl sitting on the ground with his head between her legs, blowing up the splint, all under the lights in front of bleachers full of spectators. It was all very innocent, but it didn't look too good. We hustled the girl into the ambulance and left. Nothing was ever said about it. But I sure do think about it and laugh, even today.

The stories about him are many. He did have a big problem. He was a smoker of many years and couldn't or didn't want to quit. He had a terrible smoker's cough. It was so bad that he'd sometimes break blood vessels in his face and eyes when coughing really hard. It didn't seem to bother him too much though. He went about his duties faithfully.

One day an officer went before the chief and said he was afraid for this man to drive as he might have a coughing spell and have an accident. The chief said, "OK," and said no driving for this man. Well, this didn't sit well with members of the union. We didn't have assigned drivers. Driving was a duty and responsibility that we all shared. Everyone took their turn. Besides, the cough hadn't been seen as a problem before. We voted to talk to the chief about letting the man drive again. The boss said, "OK, if that's what you want." And so our buddy could drive again.

His first shift back on the ambulance, while driving to a local hospital with a patient, he was crossing a major intersection with his lights and siren going. He stopped and made sure traffic was stopped, then he proceeded into the intersection. It was then that a car, driven by a distracted driver, thought he had the right of way and came into the intersection and collided with the ambulance. The investigation cleared our friend of fault, but it sure made us look foolish for a while.

The stories go on and I've just named a few. He never did quit smoking, and after a while he slowed down. He started to use some sick leave and finally he told us he had cancer. Things got worse and he had to retire. Our friend finally passed on and we buried him with departmental honors. I do miss him and often laugh at the stories. He's buried very near my grandparents, so I visit with him sometimes. I think, if there really is an afterlife, I wonder if he's giving my grandfather a rub down.

Memories

I remember the fire service when men were men. We wore heavy canvas coats made even heavier by the wool liners we had to put in them in the winter to stay warm. We wore rubber boots that were stored folded down and pulled up at a fire. They were ¾ boots and reached your mid-thigh when pulled up. Bunker pants were called "quick hitches." They were worn for warmth instead of protection. Sometimes they were called a "night hitch" and used for speed in getting dressed and on the road at night. They were left folded over our special short boots and placed next to your bed at night. Since their purpose was speed and warmth, they were not required and not everybody had them. They were not issued and had to be bought by the individual firefighters. We wore helmets without impact caps inside. We wore whatever gloves we wanted: some wore rubber gloves. There were not enough air packs for everybody and the new guys had to prove they could "take it" to be one of the guys.

We rode in trucks without roofs and sat in rain and snow both responding to and returning from fires, with wipers cleaning the inside of the windshield. There were no automatics so you'd better learn to shift smoothly. We rode standing on the rear step in all weather, holding on for dear life as the engine sped to the fire.

We worked hard spraying water in the winter trying to work in that heavy coat and sucking up smoke. We worked on, in spite of frozen feet and toes, fingers and hands. Noses ran in the smoke and we had those brown and green icicles hanging from eyebrows and mustaches. "Rehab" was coming outside to rest, lighting up a cigarette, and inhaling deeply. You'd cough a few times, spit out some black stuff, and you'd be ready for more work. "Air conditioning" was opening the window. In the winter after a fire, you'd spend a while trying to knock the ice off of your coat so you could get it off, or sometimes, with some help, you could slip it over your head and stand it in a corner until it thawed out. "Critical incident stress debriefing" back then consisted of the guys sitting around the kitchen table talking about the incident. Then maybe a bunch of us would go out for a few beers, usually quite a few, and we'd really talk it out of our systems.

Things are better now. We have SCBA for everyone and many departments mandate their use. We have better, lighter two-piece gear that protects far better than the gear of yesteryear. Gone are the night hitches used strictly for warmth, and the ¾ boots. We have special firefighting gloves and protective hoods to protect the ears, neck and head, and helmets with impact caps that better protect the head. The hose and couplings are lighter and the pumps more efficient. The job is still hard and dangerous, but we're protecting our people better. Smoking is permitted fewer and fewer places now. It's been banned in the firehouse for many years. The real old-timers are almost gone now, leaving better-trained and better-equipped people to do the job. We now have trained counselors to talk to if something really bothers us. Around the time I first came on the job and before, the average life expectancy for a firefighter after retirement was five years. We've come a long way.

MFFA Car Fires

Not all of my favorite stories happened at the firehouse. Most of us have a second job for our days off. I have worked at many things, but I have stayed with what I am best at. So, I still work within the fire service, teaching. Through the years at the Massachusetts Firefighting Academy (MFFA), we've used various ways to teach our students many different things. We burn straw and pallets as our primary fuel. We have since changed our methods, but we used to have a full size car up on a kind of platform and we used to fill it with straw and set fire to it to teach car fires. The students would advance on the fire we set for them and learn the techniques.

One day some years back, while we were teaching car fires, I was carrying bales of straw to the car. I had one that, in retrospect, seemed heavier than the others—not really uncommon—so it went unnoticed. We were busy with a lot of work left to do, so we just broke up the bale and got ready to burn. As soon as the "straw" was set on fire, just about everyone looked up. People were removing air masks and sniffing the air, just to make sure they weren't mistaken. They weren't. The air was filled with the unmistakable smell of marijuana burning. It was just like any party you might have gone to in the 70s...or anywhere else for that matter! The students moved in with the hose and put out the fire.

Then we took a look. It was all stems and leaves—no straw at all in that bale! Hard as we looked, we couldn't find another bale of that stuff in the storage trailer. All our straw is "virgin straw," that is, there has never been any insecticide or any other chemical used on it. It usually comes from Canada. I guess someone had a small garden in the hayfield, but they weren't quick enough before the baler went through. I don't suppose they were too happy. Guess they'd be really pissed off if they knew what finally happened to their crop!

Mongolians

Many years ago in a much different era, I was working with a man who was much older than me. He was hired at a time when the fire department recruited and hired people willing to do the job, right off the street. Many lacked much education and there was little formal training, but on-the-job training was the norm. This man fit the description of men from that era. He lacked much education and social graces.

We went to an accident involving a special education bus transporting a child with Down's syndrome. Fortunately, there were no serious injuries. Later, my partner was discussing the call, and he referred to the patient as a "Mongolian."

I corrected him, telling him it was called, "Down's Syndrome."

He turned and yelled at me and said, "Don't you contradict me, you little bastard. He was a Mongolian!"

So, deciding not to argue, I said, "OK man, you're right. He was a Mongolian!"

I still laugh at the ignorance of the people from that era and the kind of people we had on the job back then. Boy, how the times have changed!

Most Rewarding Day

The recruit program at the Massachusetts Firefighting Academy was ever changing. It was always being updated and changed to meet new needs. We used to have days when we trained in the ladder tower with multiple companies working together. That would be several engine companies, a ladder company, and a rescue company, all working together in simulated fire conditions.

One day, while doing this type of training, I was assigned the rescue company. Our job was to search the floors above the fire floor for victims. There were no fires lit in this building, so we would simulate the fire conditions and have the students on SCBA. We also used manikins made up of old hose. Our engineering department took the old, worn out hose and somehow formed it into human-like forms that we could use for rescue training. There were different sizes, too, representing large and small adults, children and infants. While setting up the 4th floor for the evolution, I placed an infant manikin on the floor and dropped an adult on top of it.

When the evolution started, my rescue company made its way to the 4th floor in the main stairwell. They did everything right as they felt the door for heat, then donned their face pieces before entering. They wore blacked out face pieces for more realism. Everybody was required to carry a tool, either a flat head or pick head axe or a Halligan tool.

They entered and felt their way along the walls in darkness while sweeping the floor in front and to the sides with the handles of their tools. They felt their way about halfway around the room and one of the crew members touched something with the handle of his tool. They checked and found that it was an unconscious victim. They performed perfectly, taking control of the victim and safely dragging it back the way they had come, out the door into the stairwell.

There, I had them leave the victim and come with me to the street where we talked about the job they just did. I complimented them on a job well done. I said, "I want you all to know that you did a good job. You did nothing wrong. Now come with me." I took them up the stairs again and entered the room on the 4th floor. We walked to where they had found the victim and I showed them the baby, still on the floor. I asked if they thought it would be unusual for a mother to lie on top of her baby to protect it. They all agreed that it would be something likely to happen. I told them that they did their job well, but that they should take that last second to sweep the floor once more, quickly, just to be sure there was nothing else there. I told them they would kick themselves in the ass for the rest of their lives if another crew found that baby dead in a secondary search after they had rescued the mother from the same room. There was one recruit, the team leader, who I was told, was really bothered by them having missed the baby. Lesson learned.

About a month later, we were doing a similar drill. I set up the floor the same way: baby on the floor with mother on top. As luck would have it, I had the same group as my rescue company. We went in and up the stairs, felt the door and made entry properly. They made their way around the room until one of them found a victim. They took the victim to the wall and prepared to drag them out when the team leader said, "Hold up." He swept the floor one more time and found the baby. He told his crew they had a second victim. They removed both and the evolution was over.

I went to the team leader and shook his hand and congratulated him on remembering his previous training and learning from past mistakes. I was told later that it meant a lot to that recruit that I took the time to say something to him about what he did. What the hell! He did a great job and more importantly, he will always remember to do that last check for the rest of his career. As for me, that was the first time that I knew that someone had learned something from me. He learned because I taught him and now he'll never forget. It was one of my most rewarding days.

Neck Breather

I've told some tales that made others look silly. Now it's my turn. One day at station 2, we were dispatched for a medical call: a man bleeding from the neck. We were first due with about a minute response time.

On arrival, I found a man on the living room floor in an ever-widening pool of bright, frothy, red blood. He was alive and moving around. I am not new on the job, and wasn't then either, but the scene presented a sense of urgency that we don't see that often. I saw that the blood was coming from the neck, but couldn't see where, so I took a large trauma dressing and prepared to apply direct pressure. That's when he held up his arm. With all that blood it was hard to see, but I could make out a medic alert bracelet. I cleaned it off and looked on the back. "I Have a Stoma," it read. The man was a neck breather...and I'm getting ready to pack his neck with trauma dressings! (*Holy shit, Batman!*) The ambulance showed up and we managed to slow the blood flow some.

What had happened was this. This was a cancer patient. He had had a tumor removed from his neck several days prior. Sitting at home, things started to bleed. I believe his carotid artery was involved. I don't know how he made out, but he had a systolic pressure of 70 and no detectable diastolic pressure when he was put on the helicopter. Not good.

As for me, what if he had not showed me his wrist? In our business, you don't worry about those kinds of *What ifs*. We learn from our mistakes and move on, much the wiser. A mistake isn't *truly* dumb unless you do the same thing twice.

Never Mind That. Just Do It!

Everyone who works at the fire academy works in a fire department somewhere. The academy is their second job. At the academy there is always a fire department scanner running to pick up fire calls from surrounding towns. If there is a fire, anyone working that day who is on that town's fire department is notified so they can leave to report to their firehouse.

One day when I was working at the MFFA, a call came in for a box being struck for a fire in my town. I left and responded to station 2. The fire was in a large house, diagonally across the street from station 2. There were out-of-town companies covering the station, so I put my gear on and walked across the street.

I worked there through the afternoon, and at one point, I was operating a pump. We were hooked up to a hydrant and I had several attack lines operating, all being fed from my engine and using a lot of water. An out-of-town company had laid 5-inch hose from a hydrant down Main Street which took much of the available water. I had about 15 lbs. showing on my intake gauge, meaning I had no more water left to give. A captain came over and ordered me to put the gun on top of my engine into service and he wanted a big line to the front door. I told him that I couldn't give him what he requested and tried to show him the gauge, but he said, "Never mind that. Just do it!"

Well, I didn't have any water to give him, but I shrugged and followed his orders and opened the lines to the gun and the attack line. Just as I knew would happen, the hose stayed limp with no water filling it and the gun did not get any water to spray. The captain didn't end up getting what he wanted.

Ahhh, the olden days, when we had all-knowing officers and pumps that created their own water!

New Building

The headquarters of the fire department is, and has always been, located in the center of town. There is a river located nearby, as well as a large pond, and a brook runs behind the firehouse. The water table is high there. Often, after a snowy winter or during a rainy spring, the river rises and the town center is sometimes under several feet of water. The town owes its existence to the river flooding. Way back in the olden days, our town was part of the town next door. When the river would flood every spring, it was impossible for the residents to come to Sunday services. Eventually, they were granted permission to build their own meetinghouse on the east side of the river. Thus the town was born. The name was changed later to what it is today.

Well, the river still rises and when it does, water starts coming into the basement of the firehouse. Even in times when the center wasn't under water, there was often water in the basement. For twenty-five or so years, I would assist in water removal from the basement of that building.

The town hall offices, the fire department, and the police department all shared this building for many years. Then the town hall offices moved to the old jr. high school building. As our building was a bit obsolete and was never intended for the purpose it served, there was talk of putting up a new building. The talk went on for years. There was an offer of land about a mile away, but the town wanted to keep the new public safety building on the same site it had always occupied.

Then there were the design problems for a new building. Trying to get people to agree is not an easy thing. There was one prominent individual who was always writing to the local papers complaining about something. This man went as far as to say that there was no water problem on the site, and so rather than go up two stories, as had been suggested, we should build at ground level and go down. That would have been interesting.

During construction, the fire department spent more than a year in temporary quarters consisting of trailers and a temporary garage for the vehicles, while the police and dispatch worked out of the town hall.

Finally, the new building was done and ready to occupy. The first floor was made up of the fire apparatus floor, a meeting room, the dispatch center, some police offices, the cellblock, and some other police facilities. On the second floor was the fire department living quarters and the offices for the fire and police departments. The third floor housed the locker rooms and a workout room. The fire department had brass poles from the third floor to the second and from the second floor to the apparatus floor. The basement was used for some storage, the HVAC room, electrical rooms, the elevator machine room, the police evidence room and a workshop for the fire alarm superintendent.

There were problems with this new building right from the start. The dropped ceiling in the third floor workout room had water stains, indicating that the new pitched, metal roof had already leaked. There was a flat, rubber membrane roof over the apparatus floor that leaked since the day we moved in. There were also some other little problems associated with new buildings.

After a couple of years in the building, one rainy, spring Saturday, I was up about 6 a.m. doing my reports when the police sergeant came into my office and said, "Hey Capt., you better come and look at this."

I got up and followed him to the basement and into a large room. I couldn't believe my eyes. The floor was pushed up about a foot in the center of the room. There were large cracks in the floor and water was pouring in through those cracks. I went back upstairs, called the chief of department at home, and told him what was happening. He didn't seem too panicked about it, but said he would be in. I was off duty at 8 a.m. When my relief came in, I showed him what was going on and told him the chief was coming in. That was really the end of my involvement. We had to keep a pump going down in the basement to keep the water in check until the water table lowered.

It seems that there had been agreement among the designers of the building that we did, indeed, have a water problem. Well, the engineers had come up with a solution. They dug down and placed a vinyl cap down underground. Then they filled the hole with gravel, poured the concrete, and built the building. Those college boys must have overlooked something even an uneducated dummy like me knew: *You can't compress water!* Water will do what it wants, when it wants.

Well, their oversight led to damage to the building and a water problem inside the new building. This, in turn, led to a mold problem with the wallboard due to the moisture. A company was hired to take the moldy wallboard out. The problems continue to this day.

Not long after I retired, the water came back with a vengeance with several feet filling the basement. This led to moving all of the valuable things, like the storage rooms, police evidence room, and electrical rooms into spaces that had to be built onto the outside of the main building at ground level.

The elevator shaft had filled with several feet of water. The elevator machine room was under water. As of the writing of this story, the elevator remains out of service. It has been several years at this point. I heard that the siding started falling off, too, and had to be replaced.

As far as I know, the problems continue. The engineers and builders have kept pretty quiet, as have the two past chiefs of the police and fire departments who, as I understand it, were supposed to oversee the job. It's hard for me to believe that if firefighters displayed the degree of competence shown by the designers and builders of this building, we'd still have jobs.

New Tools and Gadgetry

It seems that there is something new being invented every day. From tools to toys, there is a constant supply of new things designed to make our lives more enjoyable and easier. This is true at the firehouse, too. There is always something new coming along to make our jobs easier, safer, and more efficient. Some of these things are pretty good and do just what they say they will. Others look good on the surface. Then you get one and use it. That's when you find that it's not all it's cracked up to be. A big problem is that many of these new goodies are invented and sold by people who have limited or no knowledge of what our job is or how it's done.

There was a tool that a friend told me about a few years ago. It was supposed to be used by emergency personnel at MVAs against a known danger: the sudden and unexpected deployment of the airbag while rescuers are working on the scene. It consisted of a metal plate, about twelve to fourteen inches square, that had been punched through so there were sharp points on one side. There were hooks on the other side. The idea was to hang this on the steering wheel and use the knob to tighten it up firmly to the wheel. The theory was that if we were working in the vehicle after a crash and the airbag suddenly deployed, it would protect you by punching holes and flattening the airbag as it inflated. It sounded good. Trouble was, no one had considered what to do if the airbag inflated as you were applying the tool to the steering wheel. The injured driver and/or his rescuers would get a metal plate to the head. Not a great idea.

The simpler a tool is, the better we like it. We work in all kinds of adverse conditions, such as foul weather and in the middle of the night, trying to shake off sleep. One day, the deputy chief showed me a tool he was looking at. It was an air powered glass saw for cutting safety glass, like a car windshield, at MVAs. It was a small unit, designed to be held in one hand. Hoses from the unit were supposed to screw to one of our SCBA bottles. The air from the tank would power the saw. It had a reciprocating blade that was removable. In fact, it often removed itself, regardless of whether that was needed or not. In other words, it would fall out easily.

The deputy was thrilled with this new tool. He was dismayed when I said that it was a piece of shit—too complicated. And, someone would lose the blade in the middle of the night and never find it again—when we needed it most. He said that it would cauterize the glass, eliminating the sharp edges. I reminded him that our procedure was to throw a tarp over the glass anyway.

The deputy chief wasn't happy with me. We decided to have a comparison, a race. I would use the handsaw and another man would use the deputy chief's air saw. We used a junk car that we had outside for drill. We put holes in the windshield for the saw blades to start, not something you'd have at a real incident; and the air saw was all set up, another thing we wouldn't have in the real world. On the word "Go!" we started to cut. I had my side of the windshield cut and out before the air saw was even half finished.

There it was: proof positive that the handsaw was better. So naturally, the deputy disregarded that and bought two (2) of the air saws. They were never used, except when the deputy ordered us to drill with them.

One year we got a device that was supposed to make communication easier. After all the years that I had on the job, I knew how to communicate without a gadget. All you have to do is put the radio up to your mouth and speak loudly and clearly. This new gizmo went in the face piece of your mask and would vibrate when you talked with the mask on. It was supposed to make your speech understandable. I never thought it worked very well at all. I never could understand anyone who talked with one of those things. The chief said that I had to put it in my mask, so I did. He never said that I had to put a battery in it, so I didn't. So, mine didn't work and I communicated just fine.

Once, during a training exercise, a message came up from person to person. The message was to be told to the team leader. One man in the message chain couldn't get his vibrating, talkie-thing to work. He spent his time playing with it and the message was never delivered. In the real world, it could have been something really important. Getting hung up by a gadget that isn't working and not delivering the message could have gotten someone, maybe all of them, killed.

I could go on about things I've seen over the years, but it has been my observation that the simpler something is, the better it works for our purposes. I've never liked gadgets. People play with them too much. Keep it simple and leave the toys at home.

No Pole

For most of my career, I worked in a small town with a single story firehouse. No stairs or poles to worry about. We just walked from where we were out onto the apparatus floor, got into whatever vehicle was needed, and off we went. All the towns in this area have what are called "mutual aid agreements" with surrounding towns. These are agreements to provide help to other towns when their firefighters have their hands full. This could take the form of taking an engine or ladder truck to the fire, taking it to one of their stations to cover in case anything else happens, or taking our ambulance to assist or to cover multiple calls. Because of these mutual aid agreements, I have often been firefighting or manning the station in other towns. But as taxes have gone up and manpower has gone down, we found ourselves traveling farther away to provide this coverage.

One day, there was a large fire a couple of towns away and we were called to cover their fire headquarters. When this happens, the host town will provide a pilot, one of their people who stays back to ride with the covering company. Firefighters know the streets in their own town, but cannot be expected to know the streets in other towns. If they have to respond to a call while covering another town's station, the pilot can direct them.

Well, we arrived and went upstairs to their day room. In walked our pilot. It was a man I knew very well. We talked for a while, then the phone rang and he answered. When he hung up he said, "Ready for a call?"

We all said, "Yes," and headed for the door. We walked past the pole and our pilot slid down. We all stood and looked at each other. We didn't have a pole in our station, so we didn't know how to go about using it. We ran down the stairs—to the astonishment of our pilot, who couldn't understand why we didn't follow him down the pole. We just ran past him, and we all got in the engine. I'm sure he wondered why we didn't follow him down the pole, but nothing was ever said.

No Protection

In emergency medicine, we deal with all kinds of people. There are inherent risks in this type of job, some more obvious than others. Universal precautions, that is, the wearing of medical gloves, should always be practiced. At each call, we take in what we can about our patients; their life styles, cleanliness, their homes, etc.; and from that, we try to determine a level of risk for us, the rescuers. It has nothing at all to do with prejudice, profiling, bigotry, etc. It's just a way to determine a level of risk to protect ourselves, that's all.

We once had a patient that used to call us frequently. He was a known homosexual without a steady partner. He was also a known drug user. These things alone would raise the probability of HIV risk to rescuers, and so precautions were always taken. He would get drunk or high or both and call us and say he had just taken an overdose of some medication. We would respond and transport him to a local hospital. I don't think he liked himself very much and was probably lonely. We thought he lived alone. We got these calls from him quite a few times.

Then, one night, we got a call from a female who said she was his sister and was calling from his house. She said that he had cut himself. We could imagine him possibly cutting his wrists in a suicide attempt. The engine company from station 2 was sent and I and my partner took the ambulance from station 1.

When we arrived, the engine was there and the crew was inside. The police were also there and in the house. Because of the risks, I had my gloves on before I entered. When I went in, I couldn't believe my eyes. There was blood everywhere I looked. Our patient was seated on a chair and a young police officer was holding a blood-soaked towel around the patient's wrist. The police officer was not wearing any gloves or protection of any kind. He had a lot of the patient's blood on him. I noticed a bloody circular saw on the floor. What had happened was the patient had indeed tried to commit suicide. He plugged in the saw, held it in his left hand, and cut through his right wrist.

The police officer said to me, "It looks pretty bad." I was thinking, while looking over the whole scene and especially the officer without gloves, "You have no idea how bad this looks."

I got out some large dressings and told the officer to open the towel. He did. This was not a pretty sight. The hand was still attached but the saw had cut through everything else. That's probably what prevented him from finishing the job: he could no longer use his right hand to hold the saw. We bandaged him and took him to the hospital.

The captain talked to the lady who made the call. I don't remember if the patient had called her or she had walked in on him. Either way, he probably owes his life to her making a phone call.

That was the last time we ever saw him. I don't know what happened to him, but he sure did need some help. Maybe he got it. As for the police officer, he was a nice kid and seemed to be a good cop. But he sure did display some reckless behavior that night. I wound up talking to the fire chief about him. I said that he was a good young police officer, but someone needed to talk to him about protecting himself before he really hurt himself.

No Stipend

After being on the job for four or five years, I was transferred to a group where I was to spend the next twenty-some-odd years. I would stay there right through my time as lieutenant and didn't leave until I was promoted to captain, when I had to go to where the vacancy existed. It was pretty good on the group I had just come from. We had an officer who had been around for a long time and who stood back and let us do our jobs. We had a good group of guys also.

When that officer retired, we got a man who had been promoted from another group. Things still went pretty well. We had quite a few fires during his first year as our captain and we loved it. That's what we all signed up to do. But for his next two or three years it seemed that every time there was a bad car wreck in town, one where people were killed or badly hurt, our group was working. Sometimes that got rough. We even had to respond to neighboring towns with our ambulance for wrecks where additional help was needed.

One night a car was traveling down a local highway heading west. The two young men inside had been in Boston for a night of partying. As they approached a major intersection, they didn't even see the red light. They went right on through and broadsided a VW Beetle with three young ladies inside crossing on the green light. The impact threw open a door on the VW and one of the ladies fell into the street. There were five people badly hurt so we responded with our ambulance.

When we arrived, it was a mess, unfortunately one that we were all too familiar with. We parked, got our tools, and walked to the scene. The first person I saw was my first cousin's husband who worked on an engine company in the neighboring town. He was bandaging the head of the girl that was thrown from the VW. I started asking him where we were needed when a captain on scene grabbed me. The captain told me that their ambulance was already loaded and I was ordered to drive that ambulance to the hospital, about four minutes away. I looked in the back and saw two patients. Ironically enough, I later found out that these two patients were the girl who was driving the VW, who later died, and the driver of the car that hit her.

I got into the driver's seat and off I went. We unloaded our patients and the hospital staff went to work. My own ambulance came a short while after with my partner on board. Final count was one dead and four badly injured. All because some party favors didn't see a light. Tragic.

Well, about a week later, I was shopping at a local supermarket. At the checkout, I met my cousin who was working at the store. She said her husband had told her about running into me at the accident scene a few nights before. Then she told me he decided he didn't want to become an EMT; He didn't want to have to go to things like that.

I said, "Big surprise, he was there anyway!" What the hell, if you gotta go to them anyway, you might as well collect the EMT stipend! You know, he never did.

No Thank Yous

Funny how some people are happy to fall all over you, thanking you for being there and helping them with the smallest thing. Then there are other folks. One night, my partner and I responded in the ambulance to the home of what we call a "frequent flyer." That is, someone who has some chronic problem (real or imagined) and calls often for an assist or transport. The captain responded in car 2.

This patient was a rather elderly man who had a very real respiratory problem and we usually found him in moderate to severe respiratory distress requiring a ride to the hospital. The call came in as usual, so we had no reason to believe there was anything different going on this time. Well, there was. We walked upstairs to find him in cardiac arrest on the floor, just outside of his bedroom.

The captain and I set up oxygen, got out a BVM, and started two-man CPR, while my partner went out to get the defibrillator. When he came back, CPR was continued while he set up the machine. When we were ready, we stopped CPR and pushed the button for the machine to analyze the patient. The machine indicated that a shock was needed. We shocked him a few times and did our CPR in between. Soon we had a pulse restored. We left him on oxygen and transported him to the hospital. He did not regain consciousness, but was alive when we left him at the hospital.

We were told that he survived to come home again, but we never heard a word from him or anyone else in the family. We don't do this job for pats on the back. The saving of a life is a reward in itself. But, it seems strange that no one cared enough to say, "Thanks."

No Ventilation

Ever wonder why firefighters cut holes in the roof of your house during a fire? It's called "ventilation" and it gets smoke and heat traveling upward and out through the hole. It can assist firefighters in finding the seat of the fire to put it out. Shooting water at the ends of the flames does not put the fire out.

One night, some years back, when I was a lieutenant, I was home with the family when I heard a box being struck for a house fire. I left and went to my duty station in time to catch another engine going out the door to the fire. There was a crew of three, counting me.

We arrived and found a large, three-story home with heavy smoke pushing from within and the first responding companies all working. After reporting to the commander, I left one of my crew outside and went into the basement to find the circuit breaker panel and cut the power to the building. We then went back outside and the three of us donned air masks and followed two attack lines to the third floor. In addition to us, there were three or four other firefighters working with the two hoses to find the fire.

The heat was brutal and the smoke very thick. The only thing that could be seen was the flames as they flashed up around the walls, seemingly coming from below us. We moved around wetting the flames when they broke through, but they would always pop back up again. The smoke was so thick we couldn't really see to work, and the heat was sapping strength and increasing our breathing rate.

I remember crawling across the floor and making it to a large window overlooking the street and wondering why they weren't opening the roof. I seem to remember a call to open the roof, but it didn't get done. After what seemed like an eternity of futile work, our air began to run low and we all had to come back out to the street. We took the hoses with us, and by the time we were prepared to go back up, it was not safe to do so.

I, myself, with another man, finally opened the roof from the aerial ladder with an axe right above those windows that I had looked out of some fifteen or twenty minutes before. They were now full of fire.

After a long hard fight, we were able to bring things under control and put the fire out, but with considerable damage to the house. I wasn't in charge and not privy to the decision-making process, so I can't say why the roof hadn't been opened and I can't say with 100% surety that things would have been better with less damage had the roof been opened when we were on the third floor. But it sure would have made our job easier and maybe, just maybe, we could have found the fire and put it out that much earlier.

No Water on Magnesium Fires

Back in the olden days when we used to do our own dispatching, I was the dispatcher when the phone rang early one morning. It was a call to the sand pit by the high school for a car fire. This sand pit was one of the favorite places of car thieves to take the stolen vehicles and set them on fire. I know I sent the engine from station 1 and I can't recall whether or not I sent the engine from station 2. I guess the engine crew found a VW Rabbit pretty well involved in fire. They took the attack line and hit the fire and then forced the hood open and played the water stream onto the burning engine compartment.

I'm told there was a lot of loud popping, the fire flared up, and sparks were everywhere. Who knew the VW Rabbit's engine block was made of magnesium? Certainly not us! They had to babysit the fire until it burned out, and that took a while. We all knew that you don't fight flammable metal fires with water. Problem was that we didn't know there was any flammable metal there. Not long after that, two Purple-K fire extinguishers appeared. These were special extinguishers for metal fires. I don't recall ever having used one of them but we had them just in case.

Oh Man, That Hurt!

One of the many things I did as part time work on my days off was work at the state firefighting academy. Another man working there, and a very good friend of mine, worked on a ladder company in a city in the central part of the state. We often told stories about our job and it was a good way to pick up pointers on things that we don't see every day in our own communities.

One night, a neighboring town had a large fire and called us for mutual aid. It was in a large building in the center of their town. The buildings were close together and the fire was extending to other buildings. The fire had gone to four alarms and there were firefighters from many area departments working there.

One the buildings in danger contained an old theater that hadn't been used for some time. A group of us was ordered into the old theater to check for fire in that building. The only way you can tell for sure whether or not there is any fire is to open the appropriate walls and the ceiling. Some of us went to work on the wall adjacent to the fire building with long pike poles. I had a long pike and went to work on the ceiling with several others.

It was an ornate, plaster ceiling. I've pulled many ceilings before, but they are not usually this fancy. My pike was about ten feet long. I wound up and forcefully stabbed upwards. Suddenly, I thought my arms were coming apart. The pain shot from my shoulders down through my elbows and to my wrists. I looked up and saw that the ceiling was hardly scratched. I took a break to catch my breath. That's when I was told that it wasn't plaster—it was metal! I had never had to pull one of those before. It takes work. You have to start at an edge and try to bend it up so you can get the pike in behind it and pull down the sheet of tin.

The next week, back at the academy, I told my friend, the ladder man, what had happened. He just broke up laughing when I told him that I had tried to stab through the ceiling at first. Through his laughter, he told me that he sees them all the time. It is second nature to him.

Oh well, I saw my first one that night, learned something new, and gave my friend a good laugh to boot. I'm still not sure my arms have recovered from that shock.

Old Enough to Buy

Working one night, years ago at station 2, we were dispatched to a motor vehicle accident in our district right on the line with a neighboring town. We got there in about a minute and found a VW Beetle off the road against a utility pole. There were three young men in the vehicle, two in the front and one in the back. There was front-end damage to the car, but not too bad, and the boys inside seemed to be banged up a bit, but were in pretty good shape, that is, all but the front passenger. With the wearing of seatbelts not being law at that time, no one was wearing them. The front passenger had hit the dashboard and windshield with his head during the collision. We extricated this victim and properly immobilized his spine and sent him to the hospital. As I recall, the other two were treated for minor injuries and transported also.

We were told that the three had been out driving around and having a few beers. The driver and the back seat passenger were not old enough to buy the beer. The front seat passenger was. We later found that that front seat passenger died from his injuries. He made a mistake and paid dearly for it.

Old Habits

On vacation last summer, I went to an ice cream shop with my family. It was a hot day, so we sat at an outside table. We were just across the road from the local fire station, which had the doors open. As we ate our ice cream, suddenly the tone alert in the firehouse sounded, signaling that they had a run. Hearing the tone from across the street, my head snapped around toward the firehouse and I instinctively started to get up from my seat. I suddenly realized what was happening. I looked at my wife, who was sitting with a patient, knowing smile on her face. Then I sat back down. After more than thirty years of conditioning, I guess old habits die hard.

One of Our Own

Firefighters are a special breed. They apply for, and work hard to get on the job. Then they go to school to learn the basics of their craft. The education continues for their whole career which is spent in service to their fellow man. The firefighters are not immune from illness or injury. Nothing brings firefighters together like when something happens to one of our own.

One night, I was working as the lieutenant on engine 2. It had been a relatively quiet night shift. We had gone to bed, and though you never really sleep well at the firehouse, it wasn't too bad. Sometime in the early morning, I was awakened by the dispatcher over the department radio through the speaker on the wall. The ambulance was en route to the hospital. I thought to myself, "Holy Shit, I missed a call!" I was wondering how I could have slept through the alert tone. The telephone rang and I answered it. It was the dispatch office. They said the ambulance was going to the hospital and they would be passing by our firehouse. I was asked to have my partner meet them out front by the street.

Well, my partner was already up and getting dressed. I told him what was going on. When we were dressed, we both went outside to wait for the ambulance. It soon pulled up and stopped. As my partner entered the back to assist, I looked and saw one of our own, a shift-mate on the stretcher. He was clearly in major distress with what seemed to be chest pain. With the additional help on board, the ambulance left for the hospital.

The patient had been on duty with us. He'd been in bed when he woke with severe chest pain. He went to another firefighter's room, knocked on the door, and asked to be taken to the hospital. They put him in the ambulance and off they went, while the dispatcher notified us by phone at station 2. There were no alert tones sent.

It was not a heart attack, however. It was what we call a Triple A: abdominal aortic aneurysm. He was a very lucky man. If it had ruptured, he would have been dead where he stood.

Well, our man was sent on to Boston and had surgery to correct the problem. He was out of work for quite a while. In the meantime, I was promoted to captain and moved onto another shift. Our man came back to work on the shift I had just left.

Sometime later, it was on a weekend day and he was sitting in the day room, when his partner noticed him slumping in his chair. The man was having a seizure. His partner notified dispatch, who got help coming from the other station. Then he got a medical jump kit and starting evaluating his patient. The crew from station 2 arrived and off to the hospital they went.

I was at home and heard over my scanner when the announcement was made that the ambulance was going to the hospital from station 1. There was no mention of a walk-in medical, which sometimes happens, but there was a mention of the location being the day room inside the firehouse. Just then I knew who the patient was, I just knew. My wife looked at me and asked if that co-worker was on duty that day. She knew, too. I just felt that I should go to the firehouse. I don't know why. It just felt like the thing to do.

As I was getting ready, the dispatcher announced that CPR was in progress. That was bad news. Well, I got to the station and found that I was not the only one who was concerned. There were already a number of our firefighters there and more coming. The chief arrived also.

It turned out that the information about CPR being in progress was false. We still don't understand why that statement was made. I heard that after the surgery to correct his aneurysm, a piece of some kind of plaque inside his artery had broken loose and traveled through his circulatory system and lodged in his brain, causing the seizure. Well, our friend recovered, and because of his condition and the risk of further seizures, he had to retire. We lost a good firefighter.

We come to work, eat together, sleep in the same building just like family, and like family, we have our petty little problems. We also put our lives in each other's hands and take the responsibility for the lives of others. We never lose sight of that. You can see that when you see the concern we all feel when something happens to one of our own.

Only One House?!

A year before I retired, I was home one night when the home receiver announced a box being struck for a house fire. I didn't hear the first announcement. When I heard the second alarm being struck, I left for station 1. By the time I got there, the third alarm had been struck and a mutual aid company from another town had already come and had been sent to the fire. I went to the house phone to tell the dispatchers that I was there, and another mutual aid company had just arrived and was backing in. I informed dispatch that they were there, also. I had just hung up the phone when I heard the incident commander call for the fourth alarm. I told the mutual aid company to wait. I then called the dispatch office and told them the station was empty, and I was responding with the mutual aid company.

I put on my bunker gear, got into the out-of-town engine, and directed them to the fire scene, to where I knew a hydrant was located. We arrived and I told the crew to stand by the hydrant while I walked to the fire. I rounded a curve in the road and saw an enormous house with the roof on fire from end to end. Walking down the driveway, I met the duty captain standing next to the chief of department, who had arrived and assumed command. There was heavy fire showing from the roof, as well as the second and third floors. There were several hose lines working around the house and the ladder pipe directing its water stream on the roof. They were doing an outside attack, common practice when it is unlikely that the structure can be saved.

I told the chief that I was there and an engine was standing by at the hydrant up the street. The chief acknowledged and told me to assume the job of water supply officer, which he then announced over the radio. That meant that I was responsible for getting as much water to the fire scene as possible. I took a quick look around to see the current use of the water supply. There were already two 4-inch supply lines running down the driveway to supply the ladder's gun and an engine with water. I quickly started back to where I had left the crew when I saw a retired firefighter from our department, standing nearby and watching. I asked him to relay a message to the engine company by the hydrant: I needed them to stretch another 4-inch line down the driveway and then hook up to the hydrant to feed their line. We had all the neighborhood hydrants in use and three big supply lines going down the driveway. There were no other water sources available. We had roughly 3000 gallons per minute going onto the fire, but we were barely making any headway.

After a while, a large section of the center of the house collapsed. It was a long fight, but we eventually got the fire under control and put out. We lost the center of the house but managed to save much of both ends, so there was something to rebuild.

As I remember, what had happened was that the fire alarms sounded inside the home. The lady of the house ran up the street to a neighbor and called the fire department. The captain in car 2 and the engine from station 1 arrived first. The engine from station 2 was responding from between four and five miles away. Upon arrival, the captain found a huge three-story house with internal alarms sounding and no smoke showing. He entered and made his way to the third floor, checking for any trouble. He didn't find any problem at first, but when he turned to walk back downstairs again, he noticed smoke puffing down from around the trap door for the pull-down attic stairs. By the time he got back out to the driveway, the first engine was arriving and there was smoke pushing out from under the eaves. He ordered an attack line brought upstairs and ordered a second alarm struck. He soon ordered a third alarm. Soon after that, the fire broke through the roof and he ordered a fourth alarm struck.

The house was huge, probably the largest house fire I've seen in my time on that job. It seems that the fire had started in the attic; however, I don't recall exactly what started it. By the time the fire department got there, the attic was well involved in fire. The fact is that with a house of that size and with that amount of fire, there was a problem right away. We were a small department. The job, at times like these, is very labor intensive, and with only six firefighters on duty to make the first attack, we had already lost the race. Once enough help had arrived, we were able to save part of it, but it was estimated to be a five million dollar loss. Five million dollars for just one house!

Thanks to the chief's announcing over the radio that I was the water supply officer, I was tormented at the hands of my brother instructors at the fire academy. I was told that the talk was that we would have saved that house, if the water supply officer hadn't been such an incompetent.

It was rumored that while the fire was still burning, the man who owned the house walked down the street to talk to a neighbor and made an offer to buy his house. The neighbor's house had not been up for sale before that, but the price must have been right because he accepted the offer. The man wrote a check for that house that night.

I found the rumor to be true when, two days later, I did the smoke detector inspection for the property sale. Wow! A five million dollar loss and he walks down the street and writes a check for his neighbor's house *that night*, plus he rebuilt after the fire, even bigger than before. He must work for a *really big* fire department! I wonder if they're taking applications.

Oops...Wrong Town!

I was off duty and working at a private ambulance company one day. I was working with my usual partner, a part-time, off duty firefighter also. We both were well experienced and knew our way around pretty well. We were sent to a Boston hospital to get an elderly male patient and return him to Lawrence Memorial Hospital. The patient had dementia and didn't respond to anything. We got him on the stretcher and put him in the ambulance and started out.

My partner was driving, but neither one of us had ever been to Lawrence Memorial before, but no matter. We'd find it after we got to the town. Well, we got to Lawrence and looked around. We even asked directions. No one had ever heard of Lawrence Memorial.

Frustrated, we called our dispatch center. I identified myself to the dispatcher and told him we had a problem. The dispatcher said, "You went to Lawrence, didn't you?"

I said, "Well, yes."

He then told me that Lawrence Memorial Hospital was in Medford.

Of course! How could we be so dumb? Of course it was in Medford! Maybe we should have checked before we left, I'll concede that. But who the hell would ever think that Lawrence Memorial would be anyplace but Lawrence? It's a good thing our patient didn't know the difference!

Paint Brushes

I have often told my recruit firefighters that if people ever stop doing stupid things, we're all going to be out of work. A prime example of what I mean happened when a resident of town finished doing some painting in his home. He had used oil paint and wanted to clean his brushes. He had the idea that the brushes clean better if you heat the paint thinner. OK, then.

He poured the thinner in a pot, put the brushes in, placed the pot on the gas stove, and turned on the flame. Now, I don't know if heating the thinner works or not, but I don't think putting a flammable liquid in an open pot over an open flame is a great idea.

Well, we got the call for a fire in the kitchen at that address. We arrived to find the man outside with the doors open, airing out the smoke. Inside we found a lot of soot and those black cobwebs hanging from the ceiling. The thinner had heated and vaporized until it hit the flammable range, flashed and went out. Other than a mess to clean up, there was no real damage.

How was the man, you ask? Well, other than what amounted to a sunburn on his face, no eyebrows, and a hairline that started somewhat higher on his forehead, he was none the worse for wear. He was very lucky…and perhaps somewhat smarter.

Painted Toenails

Many years ago, I was working a day shift. It was late morning when we were called with the ambulance to a report of a man down on a sidewalk in the north end of town. It was one of those newer sidewalks that had been built well off the road and through the woods so it could not really be seen from the street. A jogger had found the man unconscious and unresponsive lying on the sidewalk.

We arrived in the ambulance and found the man to be in cardiac arrest. The way he was dressed, it looked like he, too, had been a jogger. It appeared that he had had a heart attack and had fallen to the ground. This was in the era before paramedics and SAEDs. We were basic EMTs. We began CPR while still on the sidewalk, then got him into the ambulance to begin transport with CPR in progress.

At the hospital emergency room, things happen just like on TV. CPR is continued while the patient is undressed and IVs started and medication administered. As he was undressed, we couldn't help but notice that his toenails were painted pink. Nobody said anything about it, but it could not be missed.

Unfortunately, the patient did not survive, as was so often the case at that time. Mother always said to always wear clean underwear in case you have to go to the hospital. Maybe she should have expanded on that a bit.

Panic

Panic is an awesome thing...never good. Panic can, and often does, do more damage than the emergency that caused it. It can make you forget where you are and how to get out of your home when it's on fire. It makes people think irrationally and confuses a situation. It's even worse when those who you call for help, the professionals, panic. I think every department has a few excitable people working there, but we try and direct them and let the calmer ones lead the way.

One day, not too long ago, I was the duty captain. I was out on the road for one reason or another when a call came in for a boy who had walked into his home and passed out. It was on the north end of town so the ambulance was first due. Since I was already on the road, I arrived before them. There was a police cruiser parked in front and the officer was inside.

I took my first aid jump kit and went in the front door. What I saw was bedlam. There was a teenage boy lying on the floor, the parents were crying while yelling and screaming, and the police officer was screaming louder than anyone else. This police officer was an EMT, of lesser experience, yes, but I still expected better of him. He was yelling that the boy wasn't breathing. He yelled at me asking where the ambulance was, ordering me to "Get that ambulance up here NOW!" and generally making an unpleasant scene.

One look at the boy told me that he was breathing fine. I leaned down to examine my patient. I had to yell at the officer loudly, to "Calm down." I told him, firmly, that the patient was indeed breathing. The parents were becoming a little calmer, but they were still looking from the officer to me trying to figure out who was telling the truth.

It seemed that the patient might have been involved in some activity that included drinking or maybe drugs of some kind. He had made it home, walked in, and passed out. At no time did he ever stop breathing. A simple primary exam could have saved everyone a lot of anguish, but this was not done by the first responding EMT, the police officer. He had panicked, taking the parents with him.

I got on the radio and told the ambulance what was going on. They arrived a minute later. I asked the parents if their son was a drinker or took any drugs that they knew of, never a pleasant thing to have to ask, and received the very predictable answer. We packaged up the patient and transported him. There was a paramedic team heading to the call from a nearby hospital that met the ambulance en route.

    This was not a big deal, as calls go. As for the police officer, I got all kinds of excuses from him and reasons for his behavior. The panic by this first responder created a very bad scene in the house and with the family. It cast a shadow of doubt about the abilities of both departments. Thank heaven he wasn't with our town very long. The emergency services can do without people like that.

Partners

Our fire department has always run out of two stations. Station 2 was the south station and station 1 was three miles north and was the headquarters station. The shift was made up of six men at first. Now, with the addition of women to the job, you can say we run with six people. One firefighter at station 1 would be the dispatcher. We'd all take turns with this duty. That was until, due to rising costs, the town went to a joint police and fire dispatch center manned by civilians. This freed the department to not fill the vacancy when there is only one man out for vacation, sick leave, or whatever. So now, if we run full strength, there are three people at station 1, plus the shift officer. Station 2 was always a two-person house. For many years, there was no officer, just two firefighters. Now, with the newly added rank of lieutenant, there is usually a lieutenant and one firefighter. There are times when the manning is not quite what I described, but they don't come into the story.

The two-man house can be a fantastic place or a nightmare, mostly depending on your partner. With only two of you relying on each other, it's important that you get along and work well together. Of course, people being what they are, that doesn't always happen. Personalities can always differ, but you can make that work as long as both partners are workers. If your partner is a piece of deadwood who won't get out of his own way, things can be rough. I've seen both sides of the coin. I've worked with some fantastic people, both male and female. Yes, we had different interests, but in the firehouse we made it work, most of the time with little effort. I've also worked with others who I'd rather forget. For the most part, these people came from an older group that was working here when I started.

I was hired in a time of transition for our department. In the old days, the firefighter's job wasn't really well-thought-of or desired by many. The pay wasn't great but it was steady. Many men who took the job just wanted the steady pay and enough time off to supplement the income with another job. The job wasn't really special to them. There was no basic training for them and all training and education was on-the-job.

There was one old-timer who was very difficult to work with. He was nasty to all who he worked with and he'd do whatever he could to make you look small to everyone. No one wanted to work with this man. So when I had about two years on the job, they took the easy route: they took the new guy, the guy least likely to complain, and sent him to work with this man at the two-man house. Who do you think that was? That's right, ME. That was a nightmare. My partner almost drove me out of the job. After two and a half years, I asked for a transfer. If I didn't get it, I was going to leave the department. It was that bad. I got the transfer and so my career went on.

There was another man from that era I worked with at station 2 that brings back some memories. He was a nice guy. He was also easy to get along with, as long as you always gave him his way. You didn't touch the TV, it was his. He'd fill the refrigerator with food at the beginning of the shift and you didn't touch his food. He expected his partner to wake him up in the morning in time to clean up the mess he made of the kitchen the night before; the list goes on.

One day, when things were slow, he turned on the TV and promptly nodded off. The TV was pretty loud but I wasn't paying too much attention to it as I sat in another chair reading the newspaper. I suddenly had the feeling that I wasn't alone. I looked up and saw a man standing there at the door. He had stopped to ask directions. He looked at my partner, then at me, then at the TV. It was then that I realized that *Scooby Doo* was blaring away and my partner was sleeping. I wanted to shrink up and crawl away. I got up and took the man outside, gave him his directions and stayed out to head off anyone else who might come along.

One of the worst things about working with an old-timer like that is the lack of training. They just learned on-the-job and they learned the same bad practices and dangerous shortcuts that were practiced by the guys who had taught them. I said this was a transition period. We only carried three SCBAs on each engine and the ladder: not enough for everybody at a large fire and you didn't want to be the first one to grab one. You had to prove you could "take it." We wore heavy canvas coats, whatever gloves you wanted, and those high boots that everyone knows about. Well, my partner didn't wear boots because he didn't like them, and he couldn't work in breathing apparatus. This severely limited his usefulness in a fire. Back in his day, firefighters had the reputation of being tough and brave. However, due to the lack of protective equipment, the average life expectancy after retirement was five years.

Well, one winter early afternoon, we got a call for a house fire just down the street from our station. The whole duty shift was sent, and my partner and I were first due. Further information was that there were supposed to be two babies upstairs in the house. I put on all my gear: coat, gloves, and helmet. I also had a pair of bunker pants that I had bought myself. Back then they were worn more for warmth than protection. I had a firefighting hood to wear under my helmet to protect my ears and neck. I also purchased that for myself. I got all this on and got into the passenger side of the engine and waited for my partner. After a few seconds that seemed like hours, the driver's door opened and he threw his coat and helmet in. He then put on his winter jacket, his baseball cap, lit a cigarette, and got in.

We went down the street and I saw him signal for a left—one street too soon. I told him, "No, next one."

"No, *NEXT* ONE."

"NO! THE **NEXT ONE!**"

He stopped halfway around the turn and backed up. Then he turned down the proper street.

When we got to the house, there was black smoke pushing out from under the eaves. There were people all around, but not the people who lived there. There appeared an off-duty firefighter who, without any gear on, helped me pull a hose into the house. We tried to get up the stairs to search, but the smoke was too thick. Back down I went. Outside, my partner had his coat on and wide open. I went for an SCBA unit.

He yelled, "What do you want that for?!"

I answered, "So I can breathe."

He yelled, "We gotta open this place up."

With that, he started to break windows with his helmet. No water in the hose yet, a man inside on the bottom floor without any gear on, and this man is feeding air to the fire. Funny, looking at things now, what was wrong is crystal clear. It wasn't that clear then. Basically, I was working alone for those few minutes. The engine from the other station arrived and we went in and searched. We found nothing but a mattress burning. The babies had been taken from the house by the parents before they ran to a neighbor's house.

Mattress fires are nasty with thick, black smoke and heat. They tend to smolder but can spread. We were lucky having gotten there before it got any bigger and the babies were fine. But it sure was no fun going into that alone, especially when I had a partner!

Plane Crash

Years ago, I was on duty at station 2 on a beautiful Saturday morning in the early spring. The dispatch tone went off dispatching us to an airplane crash in the area of a pond just down the street. We thought, "An airplane crash? I wonder why we didn't hear anything, being only a mile away."

Well, off we went and arrived about a minute later. We checked the pond and the area and found nothing, not even an oil slick or debris on the water. The officer got there in the car and we started looking more closely.

After a short time, we found a yard where a man had an outdoor fire going. (This was brush-burning season.) Calling back to the dispatcher, we found that this man did have the proper permit to burn brush. However, that's not what we found when we checked the fire. He was illegally burning logs. He finally confessed that he had hoped to burn the logs up faster by using gasoline. He had poured a large amount of gas on the pile and threw a road flare into it from a "safe" distance, if there is such a thing as a "safe" distance.

The result was a loud <WOOOOOSH> and a <BOOM!> as the pile took off burning. In the absence of finding anything else, we guessed that this was what had been heard, not a plane crash. We never found the caller so we don't know what had made them report what they did. I've never heard a plane crash up close. Maybe that's what it really sounds like.

Public Outcry

Back in the 80s or early 90s, there was a husband and wife who were both very well known news personalities. They were anchor people for different local news channels. One night, while driving in one of our local towns, they were hit head-on by another car driven by a drunk driver. I don't remember what happened to the drunk driver, but the husband in the other car was killed.

Drunk driving is a serious thing and someone being killed by a drunk driver is certainly a tragedy and a crime, but there was a time when the punishments for this just didn't seem to fit the seriousness of the crime. The death of a local celebrity caused a public outcry and drunk driving was brought right under the microscope. Punishments got harsher over time.

Around the time the news anchor was killed, late one night a police officer in a neighboring town was walking in a store to get a cup of coffee when he saw a young man who seemed to be very intoxicated walking outside. When confronted by the police officer, the young man said that he wasn't driving and was staying at the motel right next door. I'm not sure what happened next, but when the police officer turned, he saw the young man pulling out of the parking lot in a car and driving away at a high rate of speed. The officer got into his patrol car and followed. The young man was headed toward the town line. The police officer radioed in and a call was made to the police in the next town.

A police patrol car from our town was parked in a gas station parking lot ahead of the young man and along the route he was taking. The first officer continued to follow, but backed off, as is the practice when the car they are pursuing seems to be picking up speed. Our police officer saw the young man's car coming at a high rate of speed. Just as the car passed the parked and waiting patrol car from our town, the driver lost control. He went into the left lane and hit another car head-on. After that, his car spun out of control and came to a stop in another gas station lot about a hundred yards away.

I was on duty at station 1. The dispatcher alerted both stations to respond to a bad motor vehicle accident. Almost everybody that calls in to report an accident says that it's "a bad one," so we are usually skeptical about how bad it might really be. However, this one happened right in front of a well experienced police officer, and they usually give an accurate report.

The station 2 engine arrived first and reported a very bad accident with multiple victims. In a case like this, we have to look at everybody and decide who was to be treated first. The ambulance arrived. When I got out, I went to the car that had been hit head-on. The driver seemed to be deceased. Another firefighter then told me that his passenger, a female, was still alive; they had seen her move.

Before I could assist with this patient, I was directed to the other car, the one driven by the drunk driver, to help extricate that driver. My partner on the ambulance was already in the car with this young man who was conscious and fighting efforts to help him. He was bleeding heavily from a head wound and had the potential for other very serious injuries. We were trying to treat the patient for back and neck injury by fastening him to a short board to take him out of the car. He was swearing and fighting so badly that a fire lieutenant from another town looked in and yelled at the young man to quiet down and cooperate. It was then that I realized that several other towns were there. There were police from our town and two others, and an ambulance from another town. I looked out toward the other side of the car and saw a police officer from a neighboring town. I also saw that she was visibly upset. It's hard not to be upset at scenes like this. You just have to focus on the job.

We turned our victim to take him out of the car feet first. He started fighting again. His twisting caused his leg to come out of the grip of the firefighter stabilizing his legs. When his foot came down on the street, we saw the thigh of that leg deform. On top of other injuries, the victim also had a closed femur fracture, now aggravated by all his fighting. This in itself is a very serious injury.

It was about this time that my partner and I were called back to our own ambulance. It was now loaded with the female patient from the first vehicle. A paramedic team from a local hospital also arrived and one was in the back of our ambulance with our patient. I got in, too, and was told that the patient had been alive but unconscious until they had removed her from the vehicle. At that time she went into cardiac arrest. Off we went to the hospital with the paramedic and I doing CPR on our patient.

We arrived at the hospital and took our patient in. Work was done in the emergency room, but as is so often the case with injuries like these, the patient was pronounced dead. The man she was with was pronounced dead at the scene.

This was a grisly scene that I would like to forget, but there are those that keep the memory alive. A relative of one of the victims started a local chapter of MADD as a result of this accident and is constantly campaigning against drunk driving and for stiffer laws. I heard that one of the assisting officers from another town eventually ended up leaving her job, not only as a result of what she saw at this accident, but that might have been the icing on the cake.

The young man who caused the accident was taken by fire ambulance to the same hospital where one of his victims was pronounced dead. They treated his injuries. He stood trial for vehicular homicide and was given a long sentence to serve in a maximum-security prison. With the public outcry following the death of one of those news personalities, there was no way this young man was going to get any less.

That young man is out of prison now. A son and a daughter were lost to their families, the career of a young police officer abruptly ended, and the rest of us who were there will never forget that night. I wish I could.

Rescue at the Bridge

We have a long river running through town, with many bridges as roads pass over. When we have a snowy winter and/or a rainy spring, the river flows fast. A great amount of debris winds up in the river and tends to collect at the bridges. One year, when we had such a spring, a dog went walking along the river and attempted to walk out on the debris field. It looked pretty solid, but it wasn't, and the dog went through and was swept under the bridge.

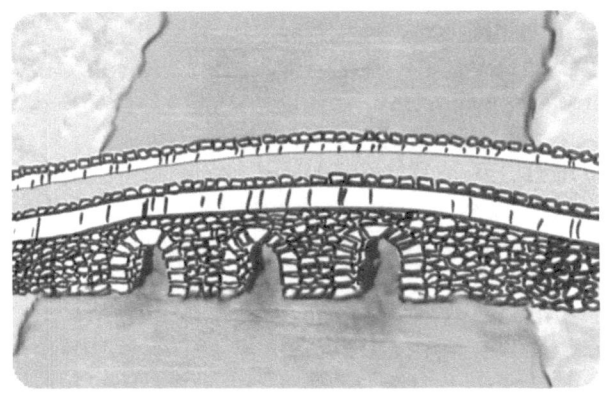

The fire department was called, as were the police who had a dive team at that time. Ideas were brought up and plans made, but the river was moving so fast that it wasn't safe to put any divers into the water to make a rescue. Also, because the dog was under the bridge and not visible, no one could even be certain that the poor dog was still alive. It is never acceptable practice to put lives in jeopardy for a body recovery, human or animal.

Finally, the captain in charge ordered quiet. Engines were shut down, radios kept quiet and no one talked. Everyone listened. Sure enough, the dog could be heard crying under the bridge. They did their best to determine where it was most likely located. Then the captain ordered the bridge cut. This was a wooden bridge that carried a lot of traffic, especially morning and afternoon rush hours, as people used this back road to get to the highways to get to work and home again. *(Oh, the Ranger isn't gonna like this, Yogi!)*

The circular saw was brought out and started and a large square cut out of the bridge. The piece was removed, and when they looked inside, there was the dog. They reached down and pulled it onto dry land, none the worse for wear. The crowd that had gathered began to cheer. The firefighters were the heroes of the day.

Of course, as the bridge had to be shut down for a time for repair, this put a stop to people's morning shortcuts. I'm sure our name was taken in vain in some places, but the dog was saved, the people were happy, and we got some of the best publicity possible for our department.

Rhoids

Many years ago, the fire department was very different. There had been no studies of fire behavior, tactics, fire loss or deaths, and there was little training of firefighters. They were just hired off the street and put to work. They were expected to learn from the other guys. The job didn't pay very much, so it didn't attract the cream of humanity.

Well, years ago we had an old-timer, one of that breed who used to rub alcohol on everything—not the drinking kind, though he did some of that, too. He'd lived a hard life, so a lot bothered him. You'd often see him walking around the firehouse with his bottle of alcohol, rubbing it on sore shoulders and arthritic elbows.

One day, he was very antsy and uncomfortable. He finally admitted that his hemorrhoids were bothering him. He went to his locker and yes, you guessed it, got the bottle. He walked through the day room to the bathroom. There were no witnesses, but I guess he dropped trou and poured the alcohol onto his lower back and let it run down. Well, they could hear his screaming from the gas station across the street as he flew out of the bathroom and ran around, fanning his backside. He quieted down after a while. I never saw anyone do anything quite like that before—or since.

The guys from that era have long since left the job, and many have left this world. A few left a lasting impression on us younger guys. Now you know what people did before Tucks® pads—and just why they were invented.

SAED

It seems like every place you go, you see automatic defibrillators mounted on the walls. The original machines were *semi*-automatic units designed to be used by basic EMTs in the field. The machines had proven their worth many times. But they were new, and needless to say, expensive. The chief of my fire department did not have the money for them in his budget and the town refused to appropriate the money for us to get any defibrillators. Plus, we had an executive secretary who for some reason disliked the fire department and vowed to make cuts in the fire department budget.

So, two other firefighters and I began a campaign to raise the money to purchase SAEDs for our department. We solicited private donations from citizens, and started a blitz in the newspapers. We also entertained an executive from a large corporation in town, with coffee, snacks, and a demonstration with a borrowed defibrillator. When the demonstration was over, that executive was very impressed and made a donation in the name of her company that completely covered the cost of purchasing one machine. In a surprisingly short period of time, we raised enough money to buy two SAEDs and some supplies to start, as well as special "skin" for our manikin so we could train with the SAED.

We then spoke to the members of the fire department about the training to certify in using the SAEDs. It was pointed out that we could make ourselves more valuable to the town and that SAED certification could, and probably would, increase the EMT stipend we received in the future. We got the whole department to agree to train and certify with the defibrillators *without* compensation for their time.

At a town selectman's meeting one night, we presented the whole package: more than twenty-four certified people, all the equipment, and signed agreements with medical control (to work under the authority of a physician's license). The executive secretary was silently unhappy, and the package was gratefully accepted by the board and was immediately put into service with the fire department. Those machines have been a standard part of our equipment ever since.

Ironically, the corporation that had been our largest single contributor was the first to benefit. One of their employees complained of chest pains and collapsed into cardiac arrest at work one day. We arrived with our SAED and brought him back to life.

The next to benefit was one of our own, when we saved the life of the father of one of our firefighters. All together, it was a fundraising effort worthwhile many times over!

Santa's Eyebrows

As many locals know, my fire department has been doing a Santa Claus ride every year since 1964. No matter what the weather, come hell or high water, we took Santa out. The ride runs over three nights and a different part of town is visited each night. Santa rides on a sleigh on top of the fire engine and some firefighter helpers ride on the tailboard or in the cab. At each stop, Santa gets down off the engine and walks among the crowd. Children, and even some adults, sit on his lap and tell him what they want for Christmas.

One year, the *real* Santa was booked and couldn't make it for one of the nights. We had a guy volunteer for the job. We got him a suit and got him all dressed up with glasses and a beard. He looked pretty good, but his dark eyebrows were a dead giveaway. While looking for a way to whiten his eyebrows, someone suggested White Out. It might have been said as a joke. Understand that this guy was really easy to aggravate. He would go off like a skyrocket without much provocation. The real, professional ball-busters used this guy for practice. Well, joke or not, he thought it was a good idea. He applied the White Out to his eyebrows. When he was done, he looked pretty good. The guys just watched and smirked.

The night went well, and when we returned to the firehouse, he got out of the suit. Then he tried to wash the White Out from his eyebrows only to find them stiff as a board. Well, he went off, screaming and yelling, while the rest of us scattered and laughed. He wound up having to shave off his eyebrows. Ahhh, what the hell. They grew back and we all had a good laugh, and still do when this story comes up each holiday season. I wonder what the real Santa used in his younger days.

Sausages on the Stove

Meals can be a big thing in the firehouse. In big departments, they cook for the crew just about all the time. In our smaller departments, we'll often order out or bring our own meal in. But then, from time to time, we'll cook for the group. If you had a good cook on your group, you had it made. We had several good cooks, but one in particular stands out. He was fantastic. Fact is, if I had to eat his cooking all the time I'd be in 7th heaven, but I'd also have heart disease and weigh 400 pounds.

Well, one day we were all in the kitchen cooking for ourselves and one man was pan frying Italian sausages and generating quite a lot of smoke. We were in our new firehouse at that time, and one of the many benefits of the new station was a smoke detector—in the kitchen. We do not advocate the placing of one of these in the kitchen unless Chef Boyardee is cooking, and even then the smoke will set it off. Small amounts of smoke or even steam will set them off. We've seen them placed outside a bathroom and start sounding when someone has taken a hot shower and then opened the door.

Another benefit of our modern building was that the smoke detectors were hooked directly into the alarm system. If a smoke detector was set off, it tripped the box and set off the alarm system in the building. Each box has its own identifying number pinpointing its location. When a box is tripped, the box number is automatically sent to dispatch. The dispatcher then announces over the radio that a box has been received and they give the location.

Well, the sausages set off the smoke detector which tripped the system. Notification started coming into dispatch that a box had been tripped, and the location of the box was the fire headquarters. I ran for the phone and dialed the dispatcher to tell him *not* to announce the box being received over the radio, but it was too late. The dispatcher did the right thing. He read and broadcasted the box over the radio before answering the phone.

"Oh, ahhh...Nothing dispatch. No problem here. Just smoke from cooking." Now the whole district knew. Talk about setting yourselves up to get your chops busted!

School Fire Drills

The public schools are required to hold fire drills four times a year. The first one is supposed to be held in the first week after school resumes in September. That first drill doesn't seem to get done on time very often, but the drills are held regularly. On our fire department, the duty officer used to take the car and take care of the drills. After some years, we and many other departments got smart. We realized that it was much more efficient to have the whole on duty shift take part. With more firefighters walking through the halls and observing, it made for a more thorough drill and we could better detect when things were not done correctly. Besides, it always better to let the public see us out and doing something, instead of sitting in the firehouse behind closed doors. Getting the companies involved in those drills and routine inspections also kept the firefighters familiar with businesses and the town buildings and schools.

The drills usually went pretty smoothly, as long as we arranged it in advance with the individual schools. However, there are some school administrators who don't like to cooperate; they don't like the disruption in their routine. We once had an elementary school principal who used to resist and always had an excuse for not wanting us to conduct the drill. We tried to be accommodating, but time was moving on and we needed to get it done. So one day, the crew showed up at the school to do the drill and was met by the principal, again saying, "No." The captain calmly walked over to the pull box on the side of the building and pulled it, sounding the alarm. The principal was less than pleased, but at that point complaining would have done no good. It is the law, whether anyone likes it or not. Like many other laws of this type, this one had been enacted as a result of several tragic school fires where many children and teachers died.

There are other aspects of the laws that we need to enforce as well. For instance, the fire doors in the halls are required to be closed, unless equipped with a self-closing device which closes the doors in the event of an alarm activation. This is to prevent fire from being able to freely extend down the hallways. Those doors provide a barrier to hold the fire in check for a while to allow more time for those inside the school to escape. We often find these doors blocked open. Classroom doors can be open when there are people in the room, but have to be closed when the room is empty. During a fire drill, the last one out of the room is supposed to close the door. We often find these doors left open. We find often that the staff, especially administration, don't seem to take these drills seriously and sometimes won't leave the building. We report any violations to the school office and to the school department. Nothing ever seems to get done about it though.

Sometimes there are out of the ordinary circumstances that come into play. I remember a child in elementary school who was a special needs student. We always had to inform the school far in advance of any drill. They needed time to prepare him for the alarm. If not prepared, he would get so scared and anxious that he would be difficult to control. We tried to accommodate by giving ample warning. After a number of years, we had to give that advance notice to the middle school instead, as the boy had left elementary school. Then two years later, we had to notify the high school. We followed that boy through his whole public school career. I don't know what they did with him when there was a false alarm, but I hear it wasn't an easy time. Wonder what they would have done with him if there had been a fire.

Now we find some schools are evacuating slower than they're supposed to. I've heard that some teachers have delayed their classes from leaving the classroom to line them up in alphabetical order or otherwise delay so as not to overcrowd the hallway. If everything is orderly, like it's supposed to be, there should be no problem with any evacuation.

It has been a long time since a large number of students got killed in a school fire in this country. There are other concerns over things that have happened in the schools. Like all tragedies, the fires and the regulations they spawned seem to have become just a memory. Other types of school tragedies in more recent memory will likely follow a similar path. The laws enacted to prevent these things from happening again will be in place and will be enforced just as long as someone remembers.

Section 12s

In the private ambulance service, one of the more interesting duties that I remember were the "Section 12" calls. The ambulance attendant is given the infamous "pink paper" which has been filled out and signed by a doctor. The form is the order for the patient to be involuntarily committed to a psychiatric facility under section 12 of the Massachusetts General Laws. You never knew what you were going to walk into when you delivered one of those.

I was sent one day to the South End of Boston with a pink paper for a man who assaulted his landlady as she tried to collect the rent. There was no way we were going up to his apartment without the police. We called the Boston police department and waited more than two hours for them to come. That's OK. I wasn't going to chance our patient coming out with a weapon.

It wasn't always the patient you had to watch out for, either. We went to some kind of intervention center with the pink paper for a 15-year-old boy one day. The boy was a tough guy, criminal type, and we were requested to have police with us before we entered. A police officer showed up after a short while. He was not the kind of man I wanted to assist us. He started talking tough and telling us what to do. He regaled us with a story about a patient who got combative and how the ambulance crew ran away and he got the crap beat out of him. I've met officers like him before. They're in every group. His being there was not going to help and would likely make things more difficult. I could just see him giving the boy some tough talk and the boy would talk back. The mace would have come out, everybody in the room would have been sprayed, and the boy would have run away. I came up with a plan.

When we went in, before the officer could say anything, I started talking. I talked nonstop to that boy and never gave that cop a chance to open his mouth. I soon had our patient on the stretcher and off to our destination without any help from the police. It went better that way.

Another time we were sent with a pink paper to the lockup area below a local courthouse. A man had gotten violent at home the night before and had been arrested. He appeared in court the next morning and was sentenced to 30 days observation at a psychiatric facility. Because he had gotten violent, we were requested to bring our restraints. They were sure the patient would get violent and we'd have to tie him up. Restraints are sometimes needed, but in my experience, people don't like to be tied up and will go crazy if you try to use those restraints. For me, using them was a last resort. They thought I was crazy myself when I said that I wanted to talk to my patient before I brought out any restraints.

They opened the cell door and stood back. I entered and introduced myself. I sat down next to the man and told him what I was there for. I said the paper was signed and I had to take him and that he had to go. No one had any choice. I asked him if he would go without trouble. He said, "Yes." Then onto the stretcher he got and we left without trouble.

There was another time when we were sent with a pink paper for a teenage girl. She was sitting in the parking lot of a local hospital, making designs in the air with her finger and wouldn't speak to anybody. Her mother was with her and I spoke with Mom to find out as much as I could about the patient. When I spoke to the patient, I got no response. I tried to look at her face, but she turned away. We tried for some time to get her to cooperate with us. Finally, we decided it was time to stop this and get going.

My partner and I tried to coax her up by guiding her arms, and then she went wild. She was fighting, punching, and kicking so badly that when another ambulance crew offered help, I said, "Yes," and I stated that we would have to restrain her. It was a heartbreaking thing to have to do, especially with her mother watching. My partner was a female and rode in the back with the patient while I drove. The patient's mother drove her own car and was going to meet us there. When we arrived at our destination, we got our patient admitted and settled in, then I went looking for her mother. I wanted to explain why we needed to do what we did and how sorry I was that things had to be done that way. I hope she understood.

One truly pathetic call I went on with a pink paper was to a home in a nearby town for a 12-year-old boy. We were accompanied by a police officer to the home. We had been instructed to approach very quietly. We did and parked our ambulance in the driveway. The officer parked his cruiser on the roadside. We all walked up to the door, and before I could knock or ring the bell, a terrified young woman came out, the patient's mother. She was talking rapidly about not wanting the ambulance or the police to be seen by her son and wondering how we were going to go about seeing him without upsetting him. She said she was afraid he would get violent if he saw us. It seemed to me that this boy had a bit of history of getting violent with his parents when he didn't get what he wanted.

Well, she and her husband, the boy's father, reluctantly took us to the boy's bedroom. They knocked on the door and we all entered. The boy didn't seem to be someone to be afraid of. He was short and not athletic or muscular in any way. He didn't look like the physical type. He was, however, rude and disrespectful to his parents. As they tried to introduce us and explain why we were there, the boy just ignored his parents and went about his business poking around his bedroom. He wouldn't listen or pay attention to anyone who tried to talk to him. I was getting impatient by this time. I decided to try something. I asked the parents to leave the room, and they reluctantly did so.

As soon as they were out and the door closed, I barked out, not loudly, but firmly, with a no nonsense tone to my voice, "Come here." The boy looked up but didn't move. I then said, "Put that down and come here, *right now*!" It was clear to me that, in his entire life, the boy had never been talked to like that or told what to do. He put down what was in his hands and came over to me. I then told him, very firmly and matter-of-factly, that I had an order to take him to see a doctor. I told him that he had no choice and I wanted no trouble from him. Then I told him to walk out to the living room and get on the stretcher and behave himself. He did as he was told, with no hesitation or problem. His parents looked mystified that I was able to get him to comply. We got him on the stretcher and into the ambulance and transported him to where he was going.

I thought then and I think now that the whole trouble with the boy was that he had been given everything he had ever wanted, and had never been told, "No." There had never been any limits set for this boy. There seemed to be no discipline in the home. The parents didn't know how to be parents. They let him have his way all the time, and this is what they got for it. They didn't do their son any favors with that.

Shish-ka-bob

We have some roads in town that seem to be hard luck roads. That is to say, they have had a lot of fire activity over the years. The road in this story involves a fire in a house at each end.

At one end, the man who lived there was a hoarder. If you've never been in a place like that, it's quite an experience. One day, the man put a pot of "porridge," as he called it, on the stove and then took a walk to the Post Office. Somehow, a fire started. When he returned, he found us all there and his home was in flames.

The house was full, from top to bottom, with accumulated junk. I tried to take a line in the front door, only to be stopped by a "wall" on three sides of me, so I had to back out. I later found that the wall was really bundled newspapers, piled floor to ceiling on all sides allowing no entry through the front door. It took us all day to put out the fire, as we had to make our way down little pathways through the rooms. Finally, part of the roof caved in. The fire was said to be out in the late afternoon. Plans were being made to tear the place down.

Two days later, at four in the morning, the police called us and said there was fire showing at the house again. That rekindle went to two alarms. Finally, it was out. A crew tore the house down a day or two later.

The fire at the other end of the street was interesting, too. It was summer. About five o'clock on a Saturday morning, the temperature had to be 90° and the humidity about 98%. Man, it was hot! We got the call for a house fire. I came from station 2 and found flames shooting from the attic window, of course. Where else but the attic! There's no worse place to be working in that heat and humidity than a fire in the attic.

The headquarters engine company was inside. We drove past to a nearby hydrant, turned around, and stopped. I got out, took my tools and the end of the hose, wrapped the hose around the hydrant, and told the engine to go. The hose came out in more or less a straight line. However, it was partially in the street. A police officer on scene kept asking me to move the hose to the side of the road. This is understandable, as their job is traffic control. But this was 5:00 a.m. on Saturday. There *was* no traffic.

I said, "OK, give me a minute," as I finished dressing the hydrant then got the signal to start the water. I opened the hydrant, and as the hose filled, it danced all over the street, even all the way to the middle. At over 8 pounds per gallon of water, it was going to stay where it lay. I looked at the police officer and said, "OK, you can move it now!" He was unhappy with me. It bothered me, too—for about thirty seconds.

I went to the house, stopping for an air pack en route, and got upstairs in time to relieve the first crew, who was absolutely beat. I tried to make it up the attic stairs, but was beaten back by extreme heat. We needed to open the roof. The aerial ladder was thrown to the roof and a man climbed up with a power saw. There were three of us in the attic stairwell now, with a hose and tools waiting to make entry as soon as the roof was opened and some of the heat went out.

As it turned out, the man on the ladder cutting the hole was directly above us in the stairway. We had no way of knowing that, neither did he. We heard the saw but couldn't see anything. After cutting the hole, it is often necessary to use a tool to pound on the piece you've cut and force it out. Well, we heard the saw being shut down and heard banging. It got harder and louder and carried on for some time. The roof man was having a lot of trouble breaking out the piece he had cut.

Suddenly, we heard a snap, the piece of roof fell into the attic, and an 8-foot pike came down at us *pike end first*! It fell onto the stairs in front of us, barely missing making shish-ka-bob out of all three of us. We didn't think about this near miss at the time. We just got up and put the fire out. It was a miserable job.

Later, we looked at the piece of roof that had come out so hard. It was found to be a double layer of ¾" cabinet-grade particleboard. That's a mighty thick roof. The piece was in tight, so when it broke free and fell, it was so sudden that the roof man lost his pike through the hole. Quite an experience, now that I think about the near miss that it was. I never liked shish-ka-bob anyway!

Shut Up and Do Your Job!

As far as I am aware, my fire department, being small, always ran with two-man engine companies, as have just about all the smaller departments around me. As things got expensive and taxes went up, even many of the larger departments have had to cut back on manpower and run smaller companies. When working at the fire academy, trying to explain the reality of manpower to the recruits, I'd often single out one. I'd try to pick someone from one of the busy smaller cities around Boston. I'd ask them how many people they had on an engine company. Of course, I already knew the answer; It was invariably, "Three, Sir."

I would then ask, "One is the pump operator, correct?"

"Yes, Sir."

I then asked, "Then how many people do you have to move hose?"

"Two, Sir."

I would then point out that the firefighters from those cities who were on the initial attack on a fire were no better off than I was, even though their departments were bigger. It was an eye-opener for most of them, but not all.

One day at the academy, we were grading the recruits' performance on a hose evolution. I looked up onto a second story balcony where a hose line had just entered the burn building. There was a student outside having a heated conversation with an instructor. It seemed that this student had just been awarded five demerits for failure to remove the kinks out of the attack hose as required. We take this very seriously because kinks can cut the amount of water flowing through the hose, thus interfering with fire attack. I walked up the stairs and saw a great deal of hose on the floor with numerous kinks in it. The student was protesting his demerits. When I arrived on the balcony, he turned to me. He was whining loudly about how he was working his butt off trying to move the hose and couldn't remove the kinks.

I looked at him and said, "Don't whine at me." He then raised his voice and said that he wasn't whining, and asked what we expected him to do when he had no help, since he had only a two-man company.

When he said that, I froze in place and turned to face him, put my finger in the air in front of his face, and said loudly and firmly, "Don't take that road with me! I've been working with two-man companies for thirty years and I know what they can do when they have to!"

This man knew that he had made a mistake when he made that statement, and the look on my face made him very quickly back down. He was *still* awarded those five demerits. I could have written a report on him for the disrespect he had shown to the instructors, but I thought that the terror I saw in his face after I spoke to him was enough punishment. He didn't complain for the rest of his time with us, at least not so I could hear him. He *did* seek me out and shook my hand on his graduation day. I guess the lesson was learned.

The fact of the matter is that almost no one is better off than anyone else as manpower is concerned, and you are expected to do the job with the tools and manpower at hand. No one cares about your problems, not the deputy, the chief, your company commander, and certainly not the people you serve. Your chiefs and officers have already done your job and don't need to hear you complain; they have bigger things to worry about. The people that you are there to help have bigger problems than you do. So just shut up and do your job. That's the name of the game.

Slip and Slide

Over the years, we've worked different types of schedules. When I started, we worked both day shifts (8 a.m. to 6 p.m.) and night shifts (6 p.m. to 8 a.m.). That is 10-hour days and 14-hour nights. Our schedule was to work two consecutive day shifts, immediately followed by two consecutive night shifts, then four days off. It was a 42-hour workweek. Now many towns have 24-hour shifts; twenty-four hours at a time in the station with either four or five days off, depending on how your shifts are spaced. Other towns follow a schedule where they work 24-hours on followed by 3 days off. Just like that, over and over. The common thing with them all is a lot of time off lumped together and some of your regular time is worked at night.

Most of us work at something else during our time off. Some have businesses they run: carpentry, plumbing, landscaping, etc. Among many things over the years, I worked as a maintenance mechanic at a pool owned and operated by an organization in town. The pool started out well enough, but over the years not enough money was put into the upkeep and things began to show their age. When I worked there, they had a director who was a bit of a micromanager, but wasn't too knowledgeable about building upkeep. They would close every August for two weeks to drain and clean the pool and do any large projects. As I was a part-time employee, I usually got those two weeks off.

Well, the shutdown was getting nearer and the director decided that the locker room floors needed repainting. An outside contractor was to be hired. I was asked for input as to the type of paint to be used. I figured the contractor would know what to use, but I said that whatever they used, they should make sure it was textured because the locker room floors were always wet. We should guard against people slipping.

We were off for two weeks. When the pool reopened, I was told that the locker room floors had been painted with epoxy paint with no sand or texture of any kind. Well, the first day they were reopened was a Saturday and I was working at the firehouse. Not long after the shift started, we got a call for the ambulance to the pool. We found a man on the floor of the men's locker room with a hip fracture—he had slipped and fallen. The patient was treated and transported.

The next day, in the morning, another call came in for the ambulance. This time, in the ladies' locker room, a very pregnant woman slipped and fell on the wet floor. After that, the director ordered mats and covered the locker room floors with them so no one else would slip.

I don't recall what ever happened with the two people who had slipped. I can say for sure that if it were me who slipped and broke my hip, I would have sued and owned the place before I was done, just for their stupidity alone. Furthermore, if the maintenance mechanic's opinion means nothing, why ask me at all?

Someone I Knew

My oldest daughter was born in the early 80s. She wasn't much of a sleeper at night. She's in her 30s now and she still doesn't sleep much at night. Back then, it bothered us more. It was after midnight in early summer. We were awake walking the floor with our crying baby when my home receiver broadcast a box being stuck for a house fire. I put on my shoes and left for the firehouse. My callback station was station 1.

When I got there, the department radio was loudly transmitting a call for additional engines to the fire. As we donned our bunker gear, another man and I talked about the fire location, it sounded familiar. We thought it was the home of the family of a friend of ours. I got onto the rear step with others and we were off to the fire.

As we approached, the engine driver stopped near a hydrant. He yelled back that they wanted us to lay another supply line. I got off with another man. We pulled about ten feet of hose out of the hose bed and wrapped it around the hydrant. We then signaled the driver to go. As the advancing engine laid a line of hose down the street toward the fire, the other man and I hooked it up to the hydrant and when we heard the signal, turned on the hydrant, filling the hose with water. We then walked up the street to the fire.

We had been right. It was the home of a friend's family. What's more, though most of the family got out, they couldn't locate their 18-year-old son at first. The first arriving firefighters had begun a search and found the boy in the basement playroom, unconscious and badly burned. They were carrying the boy up the basement stairs when something suddenly let a rush of fresh air into the basement. This caused the fire to flare up and caught the men on the staircase. They managed to get out with minor injuries but the boy was critical. All this had happened before my arrival at the fire. I was stunned. This was the first time anyone I knew had been hurt because of a fire in their home. It had always been possible. That's the price you pay when you work in the same town you grew up in. It's still full of people you know.

Well, we worked through the night. It took a long time to put that fire out. It was an older home with many renovations. That tends to leave a lot of dead and hidden spaces for the fire to hide. You have to find them all and put them out. Sometime during the fire, I had strained my back but kept working. When the fire was out, we were sent back to the firehouse. My back got stiffer, and by the time I stepped off back at station 1, my back just froze and I couldn't move or walk. I went to the hospital by ambulance, was x-rayed and given medications. My wife came and got me at the hospital and drove me home.

I found out sometime around then that the boy that was rescued the night before had died. I had known this boy since he was little. I knew his family and a brother was a good friend of mine. I've never been able to express how I felt at the loss of my friend's brother. I went to the funeral and was tongue-tied. I just didn't know what to say except, "I'm sorry," and that seemed so inadequate.

Being injured and out of work for the month following the fire didn't help. All I did was think. It would have been better to be back at work. The brothers at the firehouse have a way of dealing with things by talking them out among ourselves. Anyway, that was my fifth year on the job full-time and the first incident of that type to involve anyone I knew. It really hit hard.

Sometimes You Just Have to Wonder, But You Can't Cure Stupid

Sometimes you have to wonder exactly where people's heads are at. The thought process breaks down and the mind wanders. Then people do stupid things, often with bad results...like the man who found a bee's nest inside a kitchen wall-vent and decided the thing to do was to set fire to the nest. Well, he did just that, and it resulted in a house fire that damaged the kitchen and the bedroom upstairs as well as the roof. He sure fixed those bees!

Sometimes I wonder if people should be allowed to have things like snow blowers and wood splitters with which they remove body parts, and power saws that they use to reshape or remove things. I saw a boy who borrowed his brother's Samurai sword. As he chopped at tree branches, it glanced off and sliced his kneecap to the bone.

Sad as it may be to discuss, this lack of thought and planning extends to suicide attempts. I saw a man who tried to cut his wrists with a skill saw. He got through one and realized he couldn't finish the job with only one working hand, so he called for an ambulance. We even had a man who tried to shoot himself in the head...and missed. I remember a firefighter friend telling me a tragic story about a man who attempted suicide. He attempted to hang himself. He went to a bridge in that town with a length of rope. He tied one end of the rope to the bridge and the other end around his neck. Then he jumped. When the fire department arrived, they found him with the rope still around his neck, lying on the ground under the bridge, in pain. The rope had been too long and he had broken both of his legs in the fall. Sad? Yes. Stupid? Absolutely. Funny? I'd say so. And while it may have turned out for the better, this incident showed the man's marked lack of detail planning. Sad, but the outcomes at least weren't tragic as they could have been.

Playtime is interesting too. There was the man who put up a zip line for his kids between two trees in his backyard. When he was finished, he just had to try it out. It held his weight alright, but I guess he forgot that he wasn't eighteen anymore and had more trouble holding on than he figured he would. He slipped and fell. Not too far, but far enough that he need a ride to the hospital to be seen by a doctor. He had time to ponder this as he waited for the ambulance, during the ride to the hospital, and while waiting in the ER.

Then there's the guy who tied the dead man switch on his lawn mower down. Then he stopped and let go of the handle and reached down under the mower to get something that shouldn't be there—like his hand, maybe?

What about the person who cleans out a fireplace or a charcoal grill and puts the hot ashes into a paper bag. Sometimes they'll toss the bag into the trash. I've had trash packers with their trash loads on fire because of this. We had to have them dump the load in the street so we could put it out. Other times they lean the paper bag up against the house "just for now." I'll let you use your imagination to figure out what happens next. What did they think was going to happen? Not a fair question. If they thought at all, they wouldn't have done it in the first place.

One of my own favorites is the incident where a man was planning to trim a tree in his yard. He brought out a ladder, extended it and leaned it up against a branch of the tree. Then he climbed the ladder with his handsaw and cut the branch that the ladder was leaning on. When I arrived with the ambulance, I found the man lying on his back in the yard next to the ladder and the tree branch. I didn't see the saw. The man was conscious and alert and in some discomfort, but didn't

seem to be injured too badly. Before we started work on him, I just had to take the opportunity to ask him, "Tell me. Do you feel dumb?" He answered, "Yeah, I do." We both chuckled a bit.

We used full, spinal precautions, cervical collar and a long backboard, in the event of spinal injury. We fastened him to the board and transported him to the hospital. I don't believe he had sustained any major injury. Funny though, I watched Bugs Bunny, Daffy Duck, Elmer Fudd, etc. do the same thing every Saturday morning for most of my life. Never thought Looney Tunes could be based on real human experiences!

Power tools, large and small; power toys; bicycles; swimming pools; sharp things; gas grills; fireplaces and charcoal grills; screw drivers; hammers; pencils and pens; and safety pins—some people shouldn't have anything more dangerous than kindergarten scissors, and I'm sure they could do interesting things with those, too.

It all makes for a fantastic study of our fellow man and some interesting walks down memory lane.

Speed Bump

   Back in the 70s, many communities began to convert their older school buildings to be used for a variety of other purposes. Many were converted into affordable housing for the elderly and handicapped. My old elementary school was remodeled for just such a purpose. It's a large building, three stories high. They added on a couple of small additions and it became elderly housing and came under the care of the local Housing Authority. The Housing Authority owns many houses throughout the town, as well as another elderly housing complex, and they hire people to maintain their properties. Some years ago, they hired a man who had grown up in town and was known to many. He didn't have a great reputation. He was known to drink pretty heavily, and there were stories of drug use, some of which were spread by the man himself. He worked in all the Housing Authority's properties, including the old school.

   One night I was working on engine 2. We always had fire and police radios going so we could be aware of what was happening in the area. We heard the police being dispatched to that elderly housing for a man looking in the windows. A police cruiser was dispatched. Very soon after their arrival, the police called for the fire department ambulance to the housing.

   Engine 2 also went to all medicals in town, and as the former school was about 200 yards from our firehouse, we responded and arrived in less than a minute. I was the passenger, and as we pulled in next to the police cruiser, I saw two legs sticking out from underneath. The first thing I thought was, "Oh shit. The cops ran over some old guy!"

I got out, pulled on a pair of latex gloves, and crawled under the car to check things out. What I saw was the man in question, unconscious and bleeding from the head. He was kind of loosely draped over the frame at the front of the car. I got out, came back to the engine and told my partner who it was. Knowing this man's history, I put on another pair of gloves, right over the first pair.

We had to wait to get him out because we couldn't extricate him safely until more help arrived. The ambulance got there, as well as the police chief. We used the Jaws to raise the car, a little at a time, and put wood blocking under to hold the car up. When it was high enough, we moved our patient carefully to a backboard, secured him on, and removed him from under the car. He went onto the stretcher and into the ambulance and off to the hospital.

What had apparently happened was the man had been drinking and was drunk. He went to the school housing and was standing outside looking into the first floor windows at the residents. I don't know what he hoped to see, but someone saw him and called the police. Before the police arrived, however, the man, who had had too much to drink, passed out on the ground, more specifically, in the driveway. The police showed up, and in an effort to remain unseen, the officer shut off his headlights as he pulled into the driveway to the housing. He was moving forward slowly and suddenly felt the vehicle run over something. When he got out to check, he saw the legs sticking out from under his cruiser and called for the ambulance. It's a good thing he didn't try backing up to see what he had run over. That could have been a mess. Anyway, the victim wasn't hurt too badly, and may have his drunken state to thank for that. He recovered just fine.

The end of this story is kind of pathetic though. In an effort to avoid a civil law suit, the town offered the man a very substantial amount of money as a settlement. It seems that the fact that he was run over by the police was all anyone was worried about. No one asked what he was doing at the windows of the elderly housing in the first place, or how and why did he end up lying on the ground in the middle of the driveway. I think there was an element of blame that should have gone his way, too.

Well anyway, he accepted the town's offer, and I'm certain he invested all that money in all the "right" places!

The Stain

I just remembered this one—hope I have all the details right. Working at the firehouse isn't all guts and glory. It's not all fires and heroic rescue work. We work days and nights there, in short we live there. It's our home away from home, and so we have to clean and perform basic maintenance. This used to include painting the station interior from time to time.

Station 2 was kind of overhauled (by us) a few years ago and a dropped ceiling was installed. Before that, we had a plaster ceiling with heating pipes and overhead lights all exposed. One day, the two-man crew was painting the ceiling. Things went pretty well until they found a large stain that the paint would not cover. Things like this are not unusual in a building like that. They applied another coat and stood back. Still not covered. One of these men was a painter in another life (that is, off duty) and they tried everything he knew to cover the stain, without success. They worked most of the day at it and they could not finish the ceiling, as the stain would not cover. I'm not sure if someone told them or the light changed at the end of the day, or maybe the sun rose over Marblehead, but they found they had spent most of the day trying to cover a shadow.

Still One of the Brothers

Some people take the firefighter job because they want people to think that they are something special. They don't care about the job; they just like to be seen wearing the uniform. Fortunately, most take the job because they really love the work and give it their all for their whole career, no matter how long or short it is. Once in the brother/sisterhood, you're never out. The only way out is for you to sever all ties on your own. Otherwise, you're one of us forever through the career, then your retirement. Even after you pass on, your memory is kept alive with pictures, stories, and markers placed on the grave by young firefighters who you've never known. You're all together, bonded that way by the job.

One day while I was working as the duty captain, I went to tour some condominiums being constructed on the south side of town. The chief of department was going also and rode with me in car 2. The builder gave us a detailed tour and we talked to him for a short while. Then we said our goodbyes and got back in the car. I had just started to leave when the dispatcher called us and told us to respond to a motor vehicle accident about two miles away. The ambulance and engine 2 were responding, as was a crew out working on fire alarm maintenance in the fire alarm truck. I handed the radio microphone to the chief and told him to handle that while I drove. On went the lights and siren and we made good time getting there.

When we arrived, we found a pickup truck off the road and up on a wooded hillside. The front of the vehicle was pressed head-on into a tree. The driver was slumped over the dash and he seemed to be pinned by the steering wheel and the dash when everything slid forward during the collision. The fire alarm crew was already there as was the engine and its crew. The ambulance pulled up within a minute. The chief and I got out. The chief took command while I walked toward the pickup. The chief call to me and as I turned, he pointed to the vehicle involved in the crash. In the rear window was a firefighter's union sticker indicating there was a good chance that this was a firefighter. It was then that I recognized the truck. It belonged to one of our recently retired members. There were two other men in the truck trying to help free the driver.

Walking closer, I saw that this was indeed our retired member. He was unconscious and there was blood coming from his mouth and nose. Considering the condition of the truck, the extrication of the patient went smoothly.

The two other men turned out to be off-duty firefighters from two neighboring towns. They had witnessed the crash and stopped. When they saw that it was a brother firefighter, they entered the truck and did what they could to prepare the patient for extrication.

The patient was slid out onto a long backboard, strapped on to the board and placed on the stretcher. As he was being loaded into the ambulance, an engine and crew from the next town over stopped to see if we needed help. They had been up the street at an accident in their town and heard our radio traffic. When they cleared their call, they came to offer assistance.

Our retired member wasn't hurt as badly as he might have been and he recovered quickly, no doubt thanks to the work of his brothers and the quick action and early intervention of other off-duty men. We all work just a little harder when it's one of our own, even if he's retired. He's still one of us.

Streets

As firefighters, it is very important that we know the streets in our town. In cities and larger communities, more emphasis is often put on the district the firefighter works in, rather than the entire town. In the smaller towns, we have to know all the street locations in town. It's easy to get messed up.

In our town, we had a lot of streets with similar sounding names such, as:

Oak Street	**Ocean** Road
Oak Road	**Ocean** Shore Road
Three **Oak**s Road	**Ocean** Road Terrace
Oakleaf Road	**Ocean**view Road
Oakhill Road	
Oak Tree Street	**Dursley** Street
	Dursley Road

You have to pay attention when you hear a call. New firefighters hear about a call once received reporting a fire. The caller said it was at "Thirty three Oak," and then hung up. Well, did they mean "33 Oak Street," "33 Oak Road," or "30 Three Oaks Road"? Interesting position to be in. What does a dispatcher do? Why, send an engine to all of them to check it out, of course. Nothing else could be done.

We had little songs we would sing with the street names as well as little rhymes to remember the streets by. There was a question that the veterans used to ask the new guys. "What is the only street north of a particular well-known intersection, (often considered the geographical middle of the town)?"

Well, the north side of town is well developed and has many roads. It would drive them crazy until they were told the answer. "It's Orchard Street." Trick question—everything else up north is a "Road," "Terrace," "Lane," etc., but there is only one that uses the label "Street."

Years ago, we used to answer the phones ourselves and then do our own dispatching. We have since gone to civilian dispatchers for fire and police. I remember getting a frantic call one evening. A woman screamed an address at me and said, "Quick!" Not much information to go on, so I asked what the problem was at that address. She screamed, "The HOUSE!"

Well, that gave me a good idea that it was a fire emergency, so I sent the proper response for that kind of an emergency. Even then, I couldn't be sure of what was really going on, so I had a plan-B in my mind. If it turned out to be a medical emergency, where could I quickly get an ambulance to respond? It did turn out to be a fire emergency, so no ambulance was required, but the information I had was vague, so I had to be prepared for both.

Bad information; confused, excited, or angry people; people who don't know what they're talking about; and host of other things (you'll notice most of the things listed are people-related) all conspire to make dispatching a very challenging position to be in. I have never lost respect for dispatchers and the job they do.

Testing Hose

Every year, fire departments take part in the ritual of hose testing. We did ours in the fall. We took every bit of fire hose we had and broke it into 100-foot lengths, connected it to a pump, and ran the pressure up to make sure it didn't burst. In this way, we have reasonable confidence that the hose won't break when we need it.

One year, after a large corporation in town had closed, I made arrangements for my crew to test our share of the hose in their parking lot. It was large and unused and there would be no traffic to worry about. We pulled all the hose from the beds of two engines, laid the hose out, and proceeded to test.

After a short while, a man came up to us and said, with a bit of panic in his voice, "There's water bubbling up from the ground over there!" and he pointed toward the main building. I didn't know where that man came from, but we looked where he had said, and sure enough, water was flowing freely up through cracks in the parking lot. We reported this. They wound up having to shut down the water to the buildings due to rupture of the water mains in the yard. They tried to blame us by saying that we opened and closed gates too fast, creating surges and water hammers in the old mains. Maybe so, but I don't think they had done anything to maintain that water system since that company had opened many years before.

We picked up our hose and went off to a church parking lot where we had tested hose before. It was smaller and there were occasional cars, but it was useable. We were able to test our hose there with no problem.

The way our department went about our annual hose testing was to divide the hose to be tested into five groups: Each of the four shifts was responsible for testing one batch of hose, and our small call department tested the fifth.

I was the training captain and in charge of the call firefighters. We drilled on Saturdays and I decided to have them test their portion of the hose at a drill. We got permission to use the parking lot at an elementary school. There would be no traffic and we would be out of everyone's way. We brought all the hose to be tested to the school and we laid it all out and began to test. Once again, water began to bubble out of the ground near the street and the hydrant we were using.

"*Shit*. Not again!"

Yes, they tried to blame us, and the lack of maintenance was somehow overlooked—once again. Then, just like the last time, we were off to the church parking lot to finish the job. We should have gone there in the first place.

You'd think I would have learned my lesson after the first time. I think the spirits of hose-testing were pissed at me for something. Funny though, we never had any trouble in that church parking lot. Maybe they were well connected and watched over by the spirits of flowing water...or maybe something bigger.

Tight Squeeze

In a town just to the north of us is a small pond. It is historic and has walking trails all around it. When the weather gets warm and nice in the spring, it becomes a popular destination for those out to enjoy a day in the great outdoors, especially on the weekends.

I was working at headquarters on a beautiful Saturday on one of those spring weekends. Our ambulance was requested for an emergency in a town just to the east of us. When we arrived, we found a man in cardiac arrest. I started CPR. I don't remember all the details, but at some point, that town's own ambulance showed up. It was decided that I would continue CPR on the patient in their ambulance to go to the hospital.

I was in the back, kneeling on the floor doing chest compressions, and my partner, a firefighter from that other town, was seated at the patient's head with a BVM taking care of the breathing. This was a Basic Life Support (BLS) run, as there were no paramedics at that time. We were in what I think was a "Type 1" ambulance: a van with an opening providing access between the cab and the rear.

The hospital was to the north and the route we were taking would take us past that pond. We kept CPR going with me kneeling on the floor en route to the hospital. Just as were we passing the pond, a tourist stepped into our path without looking. Our driver hit the brakes—*hard*. The next thing I knew, I was sitting on the floor between the two front seats, having passed through the small door opening, never even touching the sides. I shook my head a couple of times and got up and started CPR again as we continued to the hospital.

Unfortunately, our patient did not survive, as was all too common when we had only basic EMTs on the trucks. We did not hit the tourist. I was younger and smaller then, but not small enough to slide through that doorway easily, but somehow I did. If I had not been working that day, and since this was a very lucky day for me, a trip to Atlantic City or Vegas might have been in order. Probably not though. I think I used up my luck allotment for that day on that call.

Train to NYC

September 11, 2001 was a bad time for everyone in the country. Among the several thousand people killed were 23 New York City police officers, 37 Port Authority officers, and 343 New York City firefighters. When a firefighter is killed in the line of duty, it is common for hundreds, and often thousands, of uniformed firefighters from around the country, and sometimes from around the world, to come to the funeral to pay respect to a fallen brother or sister. This tragedy was immense and brought in uniformed firefighters from around the globe to attend funerals and memorial services.

A friend and I took the train to New York City to attend one funeral. It was to be held in the morning at St. Patrick's Cathedral in mid-town Manhattan. The rail lines didn't collect any fare. As we all traveled in class A uniforms, the purpose of our trip was clear. I had been promoted to the rank of lieutenant some months before and this was one of the first times that I had worn my officer's dress uniform.

We got to Boston where we boarded the train to New York. They had a special car for the firefighters to ride in. There was nothing special about it really, except that it was occupied by firefighters only. There were 40 firefighters from Portland, Maine already onboard when my friend and I boarded, and more got on as we traveled and made more stops.

When almost to the city, I had to use the rest room and got up and walked the length of the car. Many of my brother firefighters smiled and said hello, and asked questions about where we were from, how long we were staying in the city, and just general small talk. I was very surprised at how many of them knew my name. I heard them say, "Hi Lew," "How 'ya doin', Lew?" and things like that. I thought that maybe they'd spoken to my friend earlier.

When I got back to my seat, I asked my friend if he had talked to any of the other guys and had told them my name. He said that he hadn't and asked why I had asked. I told him what the guys had said to me and he started to laugh. I looked at him and indicated that I didn't understand.

He looked back at me and said, "Ya Dummy, look at yourself." I still didn't get it, so he told me to look at my uniform and badge. He said, "You're a lieutenant!" He was still laughing. As I had walked through the car and the others looked at me, they saw that I was a lieutenant. I was hearing, "Hi, Lew," but they were saying, "Hi, Lieut."

I guess the thought process was just a little slow. That's not the first time I felt foolish and it probably won't be the last, but it certainly is one that stands out!

Training Fire: Too Many Fingers in the Pie

I have always said that there's no substitute for experience in our business, and, as fires are down everywhere, the next best thing is training—lots of training.

About fifteen years ago, we acquired a structure we could use for live fire training. It consisted of a large farmhouse, 2½ stories with an attached barn, and a long stable. The structures were scheduled to be torn down to make room for new buildings. Normally, we would just conduct burns inside the building and leave it to be torn down. However, the chief at the time made arrangements to burn it all completely down. Not the wisest of decisions to make, but that's how it was arranged.

The training officer, a lieutenant, was to be the incident commander. Because I had extensive experience with live burns, I was designated as the igniter. It was my job to find out where the incident commander wanted the fires, then build and light them when all was ready. At the end of the day after our training was done, we planned to cut holes in the roof and open the interior ceilings. Then, with smaller fires, we would burn it down in sections, one at a time.

We had opened this training to include firefighters from the surrounding towns. I asked a man from one of those towns, a man who had worked many a live burn with me, to help me do the igniter's job. This was a man I knew that I could count on and was sure he knew what he was doing.

We were going to be working with limited water and access. We put one engine near the training building and used the hoses off of it. We laid one single 4-inch hose about 300 or 400 feet to a hydrant at the main road for a water supply.

Well, the day was wonderful. That kind of valuable training you don't get every day. We got to train with big and small fires, felt a lot of heat, got in some ladder and ventilation work, and did some hose handling. Our chief at the time decided he wanted to come and watch. This chief had previously worked in another town, and he *was* the chief, but I don't think anyone had any real confidence in him as a firefighter. His forte was administration.

At the end of our training fires, we started to cut holes to prepare to burn the place down as we had planned. We had men on the roof of the stable. The roof holes had been cut, but the inside ceiling hadn't been opened yet when the chief came out of the stable laughing loudly. He told me he had found a can with "some liquid in it" and on his own initiative, had poured it on the straw and lit it. Black smoke billowed out.

We quickly got the men off the roof. The fire the chief had lit took off. It hit the inside ceiling of the stable and shot the length of the building. Before long, the whole damn thing was burning. At the time, the best we could do was to keep it contained and keep brands from lighting other things. One of the oldest homes in town was just down the common drive and worried us greatly.

When the structure was fully engulfed and just barely under control, that's when the chief said he had to go to a meeting. He got in his car and left.

We were there until after dark, controlling the blaze and keeping it from spreading. Things did go well. Everyone worked very hard to keep it controlled. The radiant heat was unbelievable. It melted all of the lenses on the lights of the engine. If too many cooks spoil the soup, then one pair of hands, attached to an unthinking individual who meddles where he doesn't belong, can be devastating. Hope you enjoyed your meeting, Boss!

We Need to Move Quickly

Just as in any group, in the fire service some people are better at certain things than others. Some are a pain in the neck around the station, but you wouldn't trade them for anything when it comes to doing the job. I was on an overtime shift at station 2 one evening when a call came in for the ambulance at a residence. In our town, the station 2 crew responds with an engine to all ambulance calls. As this was on the south side, we were first due. Our job was to do the initial evaluation and get what information we can get for the ambulance crew before they arrive.

I was the EMT on the engine so it was my job to evaluate the situation. What I found was a boy in his late teens lying on a bed, conscious and weak, looking sick, with the kind of grayish look of someone who is bleeding a lot. His mother told me that he had a history of stomach ulcers and he had been hospitalized for internal bleeding, and had been discharged just a day before. I checked his vital signs and found a rapid pulse and low blood pressure. This could indicate blood loss. I was sure that if we sat this boy up, his pressure would drop and he'd pass out. Looking around, I saw that bringing the stretcher into the room was out of the question: hallways and doorways were too narrow. The only way was to put him on our stair-chair from the ambulance and carry him out to the stretcher. But I knew it had to be done quickly. I explained to the boy's mother that I thought her son was bleeding again and what my plan was. This bit of information really upset her, but I thought she had to know what to expect.

Well, the ambulance arrived. Since this was not my regular shift, I wasn't sure who was on the ambulance crew. My heart sank as the first man walked through the door. I knew from past experience with this man that things often go a lot slower than they should. Then the second man came in the room and I knew then that things would be OK. That man was well experienced and very efficient at getting things done quickly, and right now we had to move fast.

I filled him in on the patient's history and current situation and told him what I thought would be the best thing to do. Well, there's no substitute for experience. He agreed with my plan. They brought in the stair-chair and put it next to the bed. We picked up the patient, who passed out like I thought he would. We put him on the chair, strapped him securely, carried him out, and then put him flat on the stretcher. He regained consciousness again as soon as we laid him flat. The whole thing went like clockwork, fast and efficient. The patient was put into the ambulance and off they went.
    In a situation like that, with a seriously ill patient and family so near, things have to be done efficiently. Just about anybody probably could have dealt with the situation, but this guy knew his stuff and things went quickly and smoothly. He had a lot of experience and good judgment. I really didn't like to spend a lot of down time around the firehouse with this guy, but on that call and many others over the years, I wouldn't have traded him for the world!

What the Hell Was That!?

We get many routine calls for assistance. They could be lockouts from houses or cars, water problems, animals in the chimney, etc. We get many fire calls: sometimes for brush, sometimes for vehicles or homes. While these are all serious and there is always a hazard to the firefighters, often there is no life hazard to civilians. We go to medical emergencies that range from someone not feeling well to a cardiac arrest or major injury. Some of the worst calls we respond to are for motor vehicle accidents. Sometimes there are no injuries, other times moderate to severe injuries, and other times major injury and death and entrapment in the vehicle, requiring more help and special extrication tools. As the accidents go, there is always more of a sense of urgency when a victim is alive or suspected to be alive. When there is little chance of survivors, no matter how bad the accident is, we have plenty of time to do our job and the sense of urgency diminishes.

Late one night shift some years ago, we got a call for a motor vehicle accident. I don't remember what they hit. There was a teenage girl involved who had been drinking. She had some minor injuries and was transported to a local hospital. The ambulance returned, was put back in service, and we all lay down again to try to get some sleep.

A short time later, we got the call again for another motor vehicle accident along the same stretch of road. On arrival, we saw skid marks, debris, and torn up turf, but didn't immediately locate the vehicle. When we did locate the vehicle it was well off the road, up off the ground, and it was entwined in a small grove of three or four trees. This looked like a bad one. We couldn't see in the car because it was high enough off the ground. It was a newer Mustang with a T-roof. It was summer, so the roof was open. I climbed a tree next to the car so I could look in. What I saw was two men in the car, both had sustained major head injuries. It was doubtful that either had survived. It was a terrible scene to behold. From where I was, I could see and reach into the car. I did a check of both victims and found no signs of life. A paramedic team from a local hospital arrived and the paramedics verified that both victims were deceased. I climbed down out of the tree. The medical examiner had been called and we were asked to stand by and help remove the bodies from the car. There was no sense of urgency.

When the medical examiner arrived, we used the Jaws to open the car and extricated the two bodies, which were placed on backboards on the ground and covered with sheets. It's always a practice to further check the area for additional victims who may have been thrown from the vehicle or anything else that might be pertinent to the police investigation.

While checking the area with flashlights, a firefighter from the engine crew said to me, "Is that something that doesn't belong there?" as he shined his light a bit beyond the accident onto a driveway of a home. From where I stood, it looked like something that we should remove. I suspected that it may have been tissue from one of the victims. We informed the captain and showed him where we were looking.

A minute or two later I looked over and saw the captain. He had scooped up the tissue in his gloved hands and was running for all he was worth, arms and hands extended in front of him and face turned away. He was running toward where the bodies lay. One of us lifted up a sheet, he threw the tissue piece under the sheet, and the sheet was lowered. We had no way of knowing which victim this came from, but it didn't matter really.

(Jeez, Capt., you could have ordered one of us to get it, or at least use a shovel. What the hell was it anyway?!)

As an interesting side note to this accident, when I looked into the vehicle, the two victims were seated upright in the bucket seats. During the investigation, the police found tree bark embedded in the left arm and shoulder of the victim in the passenger seat. This would not have been possible unless this man had been seated on the left side of the car, in the driver's seat. It seems that at some point during the collision, the two men had been thrown around inside the vehicle and managed to land upright in each other's seats.

Where There's Smoke, There's Fire...Sometimes

In this job, we often run into unusual things, and every once in a while we get something really weird. When we responded to a call for smoke coming from a house one day, we came across something really strange. The house was built set back so it couldn't be seen from the main road. The street the house was on was a dead end, with new houses built on both sides. Our call was in the house of the original owner of all that property. He had died and the house had been unoccupied for a short time.

We found a great deal of smoke rising from the house and thick smoke could be seen through all the windows. The house was locked up and a crew went to work in the front and I went around back with another crew. I got in through a window in the back and found myself in a hallway. Things weren't right. There was much smoke, but no heat. There was no noise at all.

As I made my way down the hall opening all the windows I came across, there was still not even a hint of warmth. I came across a door and opened it, allowing the rest of my crew to enter. By now, the smoke had begun to dissipate. No more smoke was being generated and the air was clearing up. This made no sense. With all the smoke we had seen, we thought this place would really be burning...but it wasn't.

We met up with the crew from the front. They made entry through the garage and found the same conditions as we had. Checking the house, we found evidence of a flash of fire that had occurred throughout the house. There were black cobwebs hanging everywhere and there was black soot everywhere, even on the baseboards behind radiators. These were the conditions we found from basement to attic.

It took some work, but after the air cleared out completely, we were able to piece together what may have happened. The house had been closed up and locked. It was very tight. The 275-gallon heating oil tank was located in the garage. It seemed that someone wanted to burn the place and took pains to make sure that they would not be around when it burned. They built a fire on the floor in the garage, on the other side, away from the oil tank. Then they broke the tubing off of the oil feed on the tank, starting a small stream of heating oil flowing onto the floor. Then they left and locked the place up again. It seemed to us that the oil was supposed to flow across the floor until it reached the fire that had been built. Then it was supposed to ignite and burn the place down. The problem was that the house was too tight. The oil reached the fire and there were enough vapors spread throughout the house for ignition. But as soon as it flashed, it consumed the oxygen needed for the intended fire. That accounts for the black, oily soot everywhere and the black soot that flashed up through every crack and crevice. But the fire went out quickly.

    I know there was an investigation, but I never heard that they caught anyone. This remains one of my more unusual fire calls. We were very fortunate; from the way the smoke and soot spread through that house, if it *had* burned, we'd have had one hell of a fire.

Who Was the Astronaut?

On a Saturday afternoon one summer, while working at station 1, we were dispatched to a car fire up near the northern border of the town, about three miles away. We were told that the car was in the garage. It was a two-car garage under the house, so this translates to a house fire. I was driving the engine. We were making good time, when I heard a roaring coming up the road from behind me. As I looked in the mirror, I saw a police cruiser coming up fast. He went into the left lane and passed me like I wasn't even moving.

We got to the call and saw the same police cruiser parked out front. It seems the people in the house panicked when they saw some smoke in the car and they had pushed it out of the garage after they called us. It turned out not to be a fire, so there was no problem. We went back to our engine and I saw that the police car was gone.

That cop's behavior just annoyed me, driving like that to a call, especially one that he wasn't even really needed at. When we returned, I backed the engine into the firehouse, walked over to the dispatch center, and said loudly, "Who was the astronaut driving that rocket ship that passed us going to that call?" I told them about what had happened. They must have told the police lieutenant, who in turn spoke to the officer involved.

A while later, a young police officer came into the firehouse and apologized. He said that he didn't mean to step on anyone's toes. He still didn't get it. He thought it was about who got to the call first. What about the danger of driving like that to *any* type of call, let alone one that you're not essential at?! Not the brightest bulb in the circuit.

Winter

The winter could be an interesting time in the firehouse. Sure, we had the same type of calls all year, but being in the firehouse during a big snowstorm added a new sense of adventure to life around the station. For the big storms, we'd often put on extra help before the roads got too bad. This was done because small departments like ours depend heavily on people coming back on the recall. If the roads got too bad, they wouldn't be able to get back to the firehouse, so we put extra people on duty, just in case.

On a regular shift, we would have three people, plus the duty officer, at station 1, and just two people at station 2. With extra storm coverage, we could have a three-man ladder company and a two-man engine company responding out of headquarters. Station 2 would have a three-man engine company. If we were lucky enough to have four people at station 2, then they could run two engines, each with two firefighters. It was exciting to see, just like the city!

We have to keep the areas in front of the bay doors clear of snow. We just shovel the snow away so the highway department trucks could get it with their plows. It was always fun when a state of emergency was declared by the governor. Then we knew we'd be there for a while. State money would become available and we'd send a vehicle to a supermarket to go shopping. We'd grab all kinds of food and the state picked up the tab. We had some good cooks and we'd feed the on-duty fire people as well as the police and dispatch personnel. We ate very well.

One thing we all hated was putting the chains on the trucks so we'd have traction to get around. Sometimes, the officer would get up in the middle of the night to check on the snow situation, and then wake us all up to put on the chains. Each vehicle had a set of chains made to fit that vehicle's tires. The firefighting vehicles had dual wheels in the back. We'd put a ramp in front of the inside tire and drive the truck forward onto the ramp. That got the outside tire off the floor and we could put the chain on the tire and fasten it. We had to do this to both sides of all the vehicles. With the chains on, there wasn't anywhere we couldn't go, at least not that I found.

As soon as the streets were clear of snow, we'd have to remove the chains. Mostly we'd just unfasten them and lay them out flat on the floor. The next time the truck went out, we would drive off of the chains, so the tires would no longer be parked on top of them. When we returned, we'd just pick them up and hang them back up before bringing the vehicle inside again.

That was years ago. Now our vehicles are equipped with "On-spot" chains. These are made up of several short length of chain, attached to a spindle and suspended up under the truck. With the flick of a switch, the spindle is lowered and starts to spin so the lengths of chain are spinning in front of the tire and some are always under it. They work pretty well and have their limitations, but it still beats having to get up to put on the chains. Of course, the snow makes the driving more difficult and access to our calls a bit harder, but we do what we have to do. Besides, it adds a little spice to the calls.

Funny, but it seems that people wait until it snows to have problems. In addition to wires down and other storm related problems, people would call because they don't "feel good," or they don't "feel right." I always wanted to ask, "Well, do you feel 'wrong'?" Or, when we'd get a call for a home that smells "different," I wanted to ask, "What does it usually smell like?" but I never had the guts.

I do remember one lady who went into labor during the 1978 blizzard. It was a chore getting her out, but she made it to the hospital in time.

When a big storm would be raging, we experience a phenomenon we call "smells and bells." Citizens would smell smoke or something out of the ordinary, and there would be all sorts of alarm system malfunctions sending alarms into the station and sounding our alarm bells. That was something we all expected and joked about. Having to respond to the smells and bells during the storm was no picnic.

I remember the crew having to walk in front of the ladder truck up an unplowed street. We were carrying long pike poles to shake the heavy snow off of the low hanging tree branches blocking the street. Then the branches would pop back up and we could drive the truck up the street.

We sometimes had those unfortunate calls when someone has a heart problem due to shoveling snow. I know several people that lost their lives that way.

We also have those unthinking few who would try to clean out their snow blower with their hand while it was running. That was never a pleasant thing to have to deal with.

We would also have storm-related fires. They were the same as any other fire, except for the cause.

Power outages would leave people without lights and heat. There are the people who light their homes with candles, a very dangerous thing to do. Some people have emergency generators to give them some power for lights, food storage, etc. If that's not done right, the generator can fill the house with carbon monoxide and we have the problem of CO poisoning. I've dealt with many of those calls. Some people recovered and some didn't. That's a hell of a price to pay for a few lights.

Some people have alternative heating, such as wood or pellet stoves. If they're installed right, they work well, but they can be a problem if not done right or if they are older. The chimney pipes pass through the walls and can dry out the wood. After a while, the wood can catch fire from the heat of the pipes. We have seen that from time to time.

After the storm, there was plenty of work to do. Downed wires have to be repaired. Fire alarm wires are no exception. There was overtime available and sometimes we would just be held over at the firehouse for coverage while the fire alarm crew went out to do repair work.

Shoveling out hydrants was always fun. Some departments don't do it, but we went out after every big storm. The duty shift would get in the engines or the ambulance. The officer would go out in the car, sometimes alone, or if we still had storm coverage in, he would have a helper. We'd split up, each would go to a specific area, and look for the hydrants. We'd have a list of the locations of the hydrants and use the markers on the utility poles which identify a hydrant location, but some were still hard to find.

In 1978, before the blizzard really hit hard, the department sounded a general recall. That means everyone was recalled to duty. I remember going out to shovel hydrants with a crew of four on the engine and having to probe with long rods through the deep snow to find them. The ones at the end of a dead end street were always buried by snowplows. It was a pain to have to do, but at least we would have water if we needed it.

We had those big storms to deal with and I liked those. But the rest of the winter, with its slow accumulations of snow, the ice, slippery streets, car accidents, and the arctic cold, made things less than enjoyable. I complained about them then. Now I look back on those winters with a kind of fondness. I enjoy looking back on those times. Maybe absence really does make the heart grow fonder.

The Wood Man

Back before civilian dispatchers, I was doing my time in the dispatch office one day. It was brush-burning season and many people were calling for burn permits to burn the sticks and things that had accumulated in their yards over the winter. Back then, people just had to call the fire department, give their name and address which were recorded on a list, listen to a quick talk on the rules and regulations, and they were all set.

The phone rang and I answered, "Fire department. Can I help you?"

The man on the other end requested permission to burn. When I asked his name, he said to just put down "the Wood Man." I said that I couldn't do that. I needed his name. He said, "Just put down the Wood Man." I said again that I needed to have the name to record on my list. The man was adamant. He said to just call him the "Wood Man," that they all knew him.

That was about enough. I said, "Well, *I* don't know you and *my* name is going on the permit." I said that if he didn't give me his name, that I couldn't give him permission to burn.

He was angry by this time and yelled his name into the phone. It was a long name and it wasn't very clear to me what he had said. I asked him to repeat it. He did, but I could tell he didn't like this at all. I added further insult to injury by asking him to spell it. Then I asked for his address. He grudgingly gave it to me. Then he had to listen to me go through the rules.

By the time we got off the phone, he was fuming! I guess he didn't feel like he should have to do the same thing everybody else does. Some people! I mentioned the man to the captain and found that he was, in fact, known to many people, even on the fire department. Oh well. I didn't know him and he still had to follow the rules.

Yes, I Have One of Those

I was the captain working a day shift a few years ago when I responded to a call for a water leak. These are usually pretty simple, so I went alone in car 2. I was met at the door by a woman who told me that she was the real estate agent for this property. I guess the property was for sale, but it was still full of furniture. She took me to a basement playroom. There I saw one of the dropped ceiling panels out and a stepladder set up with a man on it, up inside the ceiling. All I could see were his legs and a torrent of water flowing down around him. The lady said the man was working for her and he was inside the ceiling looking for a shut-off. They told me a cold water pipe had broken. I don't remember if they told me how it broke, just that it had.

I yelled up at the man asking if he had found a shut-off. He yelled back that there wasn't one, yet he never got off the ladder. I turned and asked the real estate lady where the meter was. I was met with a puzzled look. She didn't know what I was talking about. I described what I was talking about, and she told me, with absolute certainty, that there wasn't one in the house. I told her there *had* to be one. There's one in every house, I told her. She then informed me that she lived just down the street and that *she* didn't have one of those in her house either.

Disgusted, yet undaunted, I began a search through the basement. There was a desk in the playroom where we were. I pulled the chair away from it and rummaged through some litter under the desk, and what do you think I found?

I showed it to the real estate lady who said, "Oh, yes. I have one of those in *my* house, too." I was thinking, "No Shit, Lady."

I shut off the water at the meter and left. This was the real estate agent?! Is this the person I'd want to buy a house from? I think not.

You Abandon the Pump?!

When firefighters travel, we have a tough time staying out of the firehouses. I don't believe that we really try. It's great showing up at the door of a firehouse in a strange city, introducing yourself, and being welcomed like you belong there. There is a bond, a camaraderie that extends far beyond the borders of our own towns and cities. Many times we collect mementos of our visits. I have a drawer full of fire department t-shirts from the places I've visited. I've spent more time in New York City than any place because we have relatives there. We go at least once a year, sometimes more. We were there much more often before we had children. We were free to go on very short notice then. I got to know my way around and I learned where the local fire companies are housed.

One day while visiting NYC, I went for a walk alone to try to pick up some gifts for the kids. I looked around some and before long, I found myself in front of a firehouse. This one wasn't too far from where we were staying and I had visited there before, but I just had to go in again. I didn't get there regularly enough to get to know any of the men there personally, but we always have some common ground to start a conversation. I introduced myself as a brother from the Boston area and was taken inside. We started to talk. There were a bunch of young guys there—well, younger than me. Yet there was no doubt in my mind that they saw more fire in six months than I'd see in a couple of years.

It seemed funny to me then, but they wanted to know how we did things in the smaller suburbs of Boston. I sat and talked and answered their questions. They were intrigued at how we managed to get things done with the minimal manpower that we work with. The FDNY responds with four-man engine companies, five-man ladder companies, and every chief has an aide/driver. They also have rescue companies and squads that are amply staffed.

When I told them that we respond with two men on an engine company, they asked if our nozzle man went in alone. I said that he did not. The pump operator set up the pump, got water flowing, and then joined his partner at the nozzle and they made entry. At this, one of the FDNY men exclaimed, "You abandon the pump?!" I guess that's something that they would never need to do there in the city. I explained that with the manpower available, I never had an extra man to stand by the pump until additional responders arrived at the scene. They were just amazed and kept pouring me coffee and talking for a couple of hours.

I was gone longer that I had planned, and so I shortly had to leave. I thanked them for the coffee and was told to come back anytime. I left feeling honored that these young "veterans" would be interested in how we worked out in the sticks. I didn't get back to that house for some time.

9/11/01 came and went. I think that I heard that every FDNY firehouse lost someone that day. Every firehouse in the city that I visited after that date had a memorial to the firefighters from that house that had been lost. After a period of time, I found myself in front of that same house where they had fed me coffee and listened as I regaled them with tales from the Boston suburbs. I rang the bell and was let in. I looked around. I didn't see anyone that I recognized. I walked around and found the memorial. Sure enough, there were several faces I knew. One of them was a lieutenant who had been so kind to my son when we visited some years before. He showed him around and let him sit in the cab of the engine and in the tiller seat of the big ladder truck, something my son had never done as my department didn't have one.

It's always sad to hear of the death of a brother or sister, but my heart felt doubly sad for the men of that house who had been so friendly to me and had talked to me like they knew me. I guess to a certain extent they did. We're all members of the brother/sisterhood, part of a unique breed—firefighters all—no matter where we come from.

You Need to Pay Attention

One night, years back, we responded to a major fire in one of our local towns. It went to four alarms and there were firefighters from many area towns there to help. When we arrived, we reported to the incident commander, who in this case, was their fire chief. We were told to stand by for orders. Well, we stood by as ordered for quite a while. Everybody else was working, but we were still waiting for our orders. Finally, we put on our air packs, got our tools and went inside to help.

We had been working inside the building for quite a while when the order was given to evacuate the building. This is done when there is little chance of saving the building or there is a danger of collapse. In either case, it is unacceptable to risk lives by having firefighters inside. My crew exited the building and walked to the rear of the building to our engine.

There were several ladder trucks there, ours included. All trucks had their aerial ladders up and had their ladder pipes in operation. A ladder pipe is a gun attached to the ladder that can deliver large amounts of water for firefighting. Older ladder pipes required some setup. The gun is attached to the end of the ladder before use, then the hose has to be attached and run down the ladder to a water source. The newer ones are pre-piped with a permanently mounted gun at the end of the ladder. The gun is supplied with water from a pump.

Our truck is one of the newer type. It has an internal pump that can pump the water up a telescoping pipe running up the underside of the ladder to the gun. Another way to get water to the gun is by using the pump from a separate engine. That engine would connect a hose from their pump directly to the piping under the ladder. This bypasses the internal pump in our truck completely. The controls for water pressure are located on whichever pump is providing the water.

As we approached, we could tell the truck operator was angry and frustrated. He was trying to increase pressure in the pipe. He kept turning up the throttle, but the pressure would not increase. The throttle was up so high that the truck motor was screaming. He was swearing under his breath when I put my hand on his shoulder and guided him to the rear of the truck. There, for all to see, was a 4-inch supply hose attached directly to the waterway for our gun. This supply hose extended down the street and was connected to an engine from another town. It was *that* engine which was hooked up to a hydrant and was supplying water to our ladder truck. The control to regulate water pressure was on *their* vehicle, not ours.

A look of recognition came over the operator's face and he walked back to turn the throttle down. He could have throttled up until the motor on our truck blew up and the water pressure still would not have increased. Ya gotta pay attention!

And by the way, we are still waiting for orders!

Yuck! Watch Your Step!

We have a large assisted living facility in town. It's kind of built into the back side of a hill so the front door is at the level of the street leading in, but the back goes down below that grade, and down there is a hospice as well as kitchen facilities. There is parking in the back, but staff sometimes park up toward the front. There are walkways leading around back. Below the walkway are two sets of large diamond plate metal doors covering the underground tanks where the sewage goes and is pumped out when necessary.

We were having a very cold and icy mid-winter and my group was working our 24-hour shift. I don't remember much about the rest of the shift, but things got strange in the wee hours of the morning. It was around 4 or 4:30 a.m. when we got a call from the police of someone calling for help outside the assisted living facility. The police department was on scene. They could hear a faint voice calling for help, but could find no one. I went with car 2 and the ambulance responded, as well as the engine from station 2. We got there and met up with the police. The ambulance crew and I went to the rear to search.

After a while, I heard a voice say something like, "Over here." We all went to a spot where the big diamond plate door covering the septic tank was open. It was still pitch black, but we used hand lights and could see into the pit. About eight feet down, there was a concrete platform. In one corner, there was an opening about two feet square leading down to where the sewage was held. On the platform stood a woman. She was the one who had been calling for help. The ambulance crew got a disposable blanket. I called on the radio for the engine to bring their roof ladder on their arrival.

While we were preparing to get her out, the lady told us what happened. She was a kitchen staff member and had been coming to work. She was walking from the front of the building along the walkway. It was ice covered and she slipped and fell. She slid off of the walk and down a small hill. It seems that a sewage service company had been at this facility the day before and had left the diamond plate door open. No one had noticed.

The lady had slid down the hill and right into the sewage pit. That was bad enough, but she happened to slide directly into the 2'x2' opening leading to the sewage. She hit the sides and was skinned up a bit, but she went right in. Her purse hit the platform and landed out of her reach. She didn't sink into the sewage, but was able to hold on to the edge and yell for help. We don't know how long she was there holding on, but after a while, she was able to pull herself up and out of that hole, but she was still trapped about eight feet below ground. She said she got her cell and made a 911 call. We didn't hear the report of a 911 call over our radios, so we must have already been on scene when she made the call.

Well, the engine arrived and brought their ladder and placed it in the hole. One of our people went into the hole with the disposable blanket, wrapped it around her, and as she wasn't hurt, apart from some scrapes and bruises, he helped her up the ladder and into the ambulance. She was evaluated and taken to the hospital for any treatment they thought necessary. Since she had been in raw sewage with open wounds, there was bound to be something they wanted to do for her besides clean her up.

We often don't find out how our patients make out. We never found out if the sewage company that left the door open was ever called on the carpet. But I do know that what we had to deal with was not pretty, pleasant, or fragrant. That night I was glad I had studied hard for promotion. Sometimes it's nice to be the one giving the orders.

My Good Friend—The End

I remember when I was about forty, telling several people that I couldn't imagine retiring early, that I intended to stay until they made me leave at age sixty-five. I did qualify that by adding that it was a forty-year-old talking and I knew that things might happen to change my mind. I did a lot of thinking before making the decision to retire from a job that I loved.

There were many factors that led to the final decision. Old injuries come back to haunt. The place and job had changed and was no longer the job that I had signed up to do. I no longer felt that old excitement when the bell rang. The schedule was getting monotonous. I had spent many years working 10s and 14s, and was never happy with the 24-hour shifts. The people changed. Many of the younger guys didn't have the same work ethic that I was brought up with. Some of them were the same age as my kids, so except for the job, we had little in common. I had to admit that I was the dinosaur and it was time to go.

There are also some other things to consider when the job has a large element of ever-increasing danger. You have to consider the old risk vs. benefit train of thought. When we are young, we never give a thought to the risks. Young people never do. They are going to live forever! We get our training and put it to good use in performing our duties with increasing efficiency as our experience builds. At some point as we age, we become something more than rookies but not quite senior men yet. We are very good at our jobs. The risks are still there, but we accept them as a part of the lives that our jobs have become. As time goes on, some of us make rank while others become the senior firefighters that officers depend on so much to keep the crew sharp. Meanwhile, the risks have become like old friends. At this point, we look at our pensions to see when we might be able to think seriously about getting out.

The job is still the greatest job there is, but it takes its toll mentally and physically. As our pensions start to near max, we think of the risks: the possibility of getting hurt or killed in a fire. Men and women, our brothers and sisters, die every day in structures, large and small. It can happen anywhere, from the smallest homes to the largest industrial buildings.

They say that fires are down everywhere. I guess I'd have to say that's true. But what about the increasing number of medical emergencies? There is the risk of needle sticks from a carelessly used or discarded needle, or maybe someone coughing in your face and you're not sure what is wrong with them. Do they have a communicable disease of some kind? What about people in general?

I used to say that I wouldn't want to be a cop. They have to deal too much with people and you never really know what to expect from them. This is becoming more of a problem in the fire service.

A young firefighter on my fire department was answering a call one day. As he entered the house, a mentally disturbed woman threw a pan of hot cooking grease in his face. It got into his eyes. He was out of work for some weeks as he healed. Fortunately, there was no permanent damage. Was he lucky? I'd say so.

Every year there are new chemicals, poisons, machinery and other things, all carrying the potential to hurt or kill. Whom do they call when something goes wrong? The fire department, of course, and they should. These men and women are dedicated to protecting the citizens' lives and property.

As my pension maxed and I wasn't going to be able to raise my retirement income, the memories seemed more attractive than the daily risks on the job. It was time to go home and tell stories; be there for Christmases and birthdays; spend quality time with the kids, now mostly grown, and grandchildren. Time to stay safe and hopefully healthy, so long as I hadn't had some exposure to something that I didn't know about over the years.

At 0800 hours on October 12, 2007, I walked into the firehouse for my last 24-hour shift. It was strange. Things looked the same, but they were different. I was doing this for the last time. I went up to my office, and as I was doing my paperwork for the start of the shift, I got a call from the lieutenant at station 2. He told me to take it easy, and if we had any calls, they would handle it. I started collecting my belongings and sorting out what I had to turn in. It was a pretty quiet shift. I got all my personal things loaded into my car, and spent much of the shift wandering around the firehouse, looking around and reminiscing.

At 0800 hours on October 13, 2007, my shift was over. The crew gathered on the apparatus floor and all shook my hand. I got into our engine 5, a retired 1953 open cab Mack pumper. A good friend, a firefighter (who has since been promoted to captain), got into the driver's seat and off we went. It is a tradition to drive a man home in the engine at the end of his final shift.

I signed on the air for the last time. "Engine 5 to Fire Alarm: On the air for a special detail." We drove across town and rang the bell as we passed station 2. The men had come outside to wave me by. We drove to my house, where my wife and kids were outside waiting. They were listening to the scanner, and having developed the "radio ear" over the years, had heard me sign on and knew I was on my way home.

We pulled up to the driveway and I got on the radio once again. "Engine-5 to Fire Alarm: Off at the detail. C-5 signing off. Thanks for the memories." I shook hands with the driver and he left, and just like that, my thirty-three year career with the fire department was over.

My retirement party was attended by a great many old friends and family, as well as coworkers from the fire department and the fire academy. I was asked to make a speech. I don't recall too much of what I said, but after the thank yous, I did say that it was time to turn the job over to the younger guys. "Here it is, guys; It's all yours. Take good care of it."

My two captain's horns on my badge now hang on the wall in my living room, along with the plaques I received thanking me for years of dedicated service to the town, the union, and the fire department. I got a special plaque from my brothers and sisters at the firefighting academy. That wall is a place of honor in my house.

I am proud to have been a part of it all, of such a class of men and women as firefighters are. I have my stories and memories and the pride of being able to say that I am a retired fire captain. I do hope that as the years go by, the young people, to whom I handed the reins that night take good care of the job. Thank you to the fire service, for allowing me to be a part of the greatest job there is, and thank you for all the special memories.

Retirement Day
10/13/2007

Glossary

0800 hours
8:00 a.m. in 24-hour military time.

10s and 14s
Once a common shift schedule, it consisted of two 10-hour day shifts followed by two 14-hour night shifts.

24s
Common shift schedule consisting of 24-hours on duty at a time.

26F
Section 26F of the Massachusetts General Law details smoke detector requirements in any property prior to a sale. On my department, the phrase "Doing a 26F" means going to perform the actual inspection to verify compliance with this section of law.

academy
see Massachusetts Firefighting Academy

alarms (i.e. two alarms, three alarms)
A request for additional help. Each additional alarm will bring a designated amount of additional help to the fire.

apparatus floor
The "garage" area of the firehouse where the vehicles are kept.

assist
see lift assist

attack line
A hose attached to the engine on one end and a nozzle on the other end, used to fight the fire.

bag valve mask
    Used in place of mouth-to-mouth resuscitation in CPR. Allows for high flow oxygen to be introduced.

bagging a patient
    Assisting a patient's breathing using a bag valve mask.

bale of straw
    The fuel used for live-fire training at the MFFA.

big line
    A hose with the diameter of 2½". Can also be an attack line.

board
    A spine-immobilizing backboard, or the act of securing a person to a backboard.

booster hose
    Hard, red rubber hose kept on reels on top of the engine. Used for small roadside fires and brush. Being phased out in favor of other hose.

box
    One of many pre-designated locations in town, assigned a number and used as a reference point when responding to a call. *See also* pull box.

box alarm
    An alarm for a fire. The location is identified by the number of the closest box.

box to be struck
    see strike the box

breathing apparatus
    see self-contained breathing apparatus

bunker gear

see turnout gear

burn building
A concrete building at the MFFA designed for live-burn training. It can withstand multiple lighting of fires over years.

BVM
bag valve mask

call
A request for assistance, or the response to a request.

call firefighter
A part-time firefighter who only reports for duty when called in to provide additional help for emergencies. In my town, they do not work regular shifts at the firehouse.

callback
The recall of off-duty firefighters and call firefighters for emergencies.

callback assignment
The particular firehouse where a firefighter is assigned to go when returning on callback.

Capt.
A nickname used to address a captain.

car 1, car 2
In my department, car 1 is the vehicle used by the chief of department. Car 2 is the vehicle driven by the duty shift commander.

CISD
see Critical Incident Stress Debriefing

class A uniform
Fire department dress uniform. Worn for special occasions.

coupling
> The threaded connection used to join a hose to another hose, the engine, or to a hydrant.

Critical Incident Stress Debriefing
> Procedure for dealing with post-traumatic stress in firefighters.

day room
> The room in the firehouse commonly occupied by firefighters when not engaged in duties or calls.

day shift
> A scheduled shift, usually 10 hours in length, during daytime hours (i.e. 8 a.m. to 6 p.m.).

defibrillator
> Equipment used to provide an electrical shock to restore heartbeat in a victim with no effective heartbeat.

dispatcher
> Person who answers emergency calls from the public and dispatches the proper apparatus per protocol.

dressing the hydrant
> Process of attaching the appropriate hoses to the hydrant.

duty crew
> The on-duty personnel.

Emergency Medical Technician
> Person with basic level of medical training, including CPR, defibrillator training, and epi-pen training.

EMS officer
> The officer in charge of all aspects of emergency medical services. At the MFFA, it is the individual assigned to provide emergency medical services for the day.

EMT
Emergency Medical Technician

engine
A fire department vehicle equipped with a pump and hose, used to supply water to fight the fire.

engine tank
The holding tank for water in a fire engine. In my town, the tank can hold 500 gallons. This water can be used for firefighting until a connection to a hydrant can be made.

epi-kit or **epi-pen**
An emergency dose of epinephrine carried by someone with a life-threatening allergy. Carried also by EMTs in the ambulance.

ER
emergency room

FD
fire department

fire academy
see Massachusetts Firefighting Academy

fire ground hydraulics
The formulas and information about water flow as it relates to firefighting.

first due
The personnel and apparatus expected to arrive first at a call.

frequent flyer
Fire department jargon for a person who calls the ambulance frequently for problems, real or imagined.

gauges
Instruments located on the pump operator's panel indicating how much water is flowing through the hoses.

general recall
Recall of all off duty firefighters, (permanent and call), to report to their assigned stations.

gun
An appliance used to supply large amounts of water to the fire. It can be used from its connection at the top of the engine or removed and placed on a base and fed by a supply hose to make it portable.

Halligan
A forcible entry tool.

headquarters
In my town, this was station 1.

IC
see incident commander

incident commander
The person responsible for and in charge of all aspects of an incident.

inside safety instructor
Instructor at a training incident responsible for safety within a structure.

irons
Set of forcible entry tools made up of a Halligan tool and a flathead axe.

Jaws or **Jaws of Life**
A hydraulic extrication tool with attachments for cutting, lifting, bending, and other tasks requiring a great deal of power.

K-12
A gasoline powered circular saw.

LDH
large diameter hose. Usually 4 or 5-inch hose.

lift assist
Helping a person up (from the floor, out of bed, etc.) or assisting a person moving from one place to another (inside their home).

line
A hose (sometimes made of several lengths of hose joined together to extend the total length).

live burn training
The use of real fire for training purposes.

long backboard
A full body backboard for full immobilization of the patient.

lugs
The raised "nubs" of couplings that are used for gripping securely when screwing (or unscrewing) the two parts.

Massachusetts Firefighting Academy
The state facility which provides training for any firefighter in Massachusetts at no cost to the individual. Many towns send their new hires through the recruit program.

master stream
A high-volume water stream from a gun or other appliance.

mechanism of injury
The cause of an injury. Determining the mechanism gives information about what probable injuries could exist.

MFFA
Massachusetts Firefighting Academy

mutual aid
The agreement among towns to provide help to one another (manpower and apparatus) when needed.

MVA
motor vehicle accident. A car crash.

night hitch
Bunker pants folded down over boots for quick donning.

night shift
A scheduled shift, usually 14 hours in length, during nighttime hours (i.e. 6 p.m. to 8 a.m.).

OEMS
The state's Office of Emergency Medical Services.

officer
Someone above the rank of private.

on air or **on SCBA**
To be breathing the air from an air tank worn on the back.

overhaul
The act of searching for hidden fire or hot spots after the fire has been knocked down to assure that it is completely extinguished.

pike pole
A pike at the end of a long pole used for opening ceilings and walls during overhaul.

pipe
The nozzle part of a fire hose.

private

Entry-level rank for firefighters.

pull box or **pull station**
A weather-resistant, metal box (usually red) mounted on utility poles or buildings around town. Contains a lever that, when pulled, sends an alarm to the fire station (along with the identifying number of that box). After being pulled, it must be reset manually by rewinding it with a special key.

pull the hook
see strike the box

put out the tone
To have a tone sent over the radio to recall off duty firefighters.

quick hitch
see night hitch

ranks
Hierarchy in the fire department. The order, from lowest to highest, is: private, lieutenant, captain, deputy, chief. Some departments do not use all these positions and some use additional positions.

recall
see callback

recruit program
The training program at the Massachusetts Firefighting Academy for new firefighters to learn basic skills of firefighting.

running card
Pre-determined assignments of apparatus and personnel based on location, type of incident, and manpower needs.

SCBA

self-contained breathing apparatus

SAED
semi-automatic external defibrillator

section 12
Section of Massachusetts General Law detailing requirements for involuntary committal to a hospital for a patient with questionable mental status.

self-contained breathing apparatus
The air tank, hoses, face piece, and all necessary parts of the breathing system worn on the back of firefighters and used in environments where they cannot or should not breathe the air.

semi-automatic external defibrillator
Machine used at the basic EMT level for patients without an effective heartbeat. It provides an electrical shock in an attempt to restore an effective heartbeat. A button must be pushed to deliver the shock.

shift commander
The officer in charge of and responsible for the personnel and equipment during a shift.

short board
A short backboard use for extricating a seated patient with potential spinal injury from a vehicle. Being phased out in favor of more modern equipment.

sign off
To inform the dispatcher that responding companies have arrived at their destination.

sign on
To inform the dispatcher that a particular vehicle has left the fire station and will be in radio communication.

small line

A hose with the diameter of 1¾".

smoke pushing
Smoke moving under pressure.

standard operating procedures
The pre-determined course of action to be used in a specific type of situation.

station coverage
To fill in for the on-duty crew while they are occupied with a call and will be unavailable. The station coverage personnel are prepared to respond to any calls that come in.

station 1
In my town, this was the headquarters station.

station 2
In my town, this was the outstation.

step
The wide, flat platform on the rear of an engine where firefighters would stand and hold onto an upper bar while responding to a fire.

strike the box
To have a box number sent through the alarm system to be transmitted to the stations in our town and mutual aid towns indicating that we have a fire at that location.

supply line
Large (usually) diameter hose from the hydrant to the engine for supplying water to the engine.

tap out the box number
To identify a particular box number using a mechanical device that generates repetitive taps (a telegraph) while punching holes into a register tape. The number of taps

grouped together corresponds to each digit of the box number.
(i.e. box number 342=tap-tap-tap tap-tap-tap-tap tap-tap)

truck
A fire department ladder truck, equipped with an aerial device, ground ladders, and forcible entry equipment (used for overhaul).

turnout gear
Protective clothing for firefighting (helmet, hood, coat, pants, boots, gloves).

ventilation
The act of opening a structure (windows, cutting the roof) to release smoke and heat to aid the firefighters in battling the fire.

walk-in medical
Someone in need of medical help who comes in person to the fire station instead of phoning.

watch room
A room formerly used for our dispatcher, now used for greeting the public and routine business.

well-being check
Going to a person's house to check on their welfare, at the request of family or friends who are concerned because they are unable to reach that person.

working fire
Fire department jargon for a fire that is free burning and still growing; pre-fire attack.